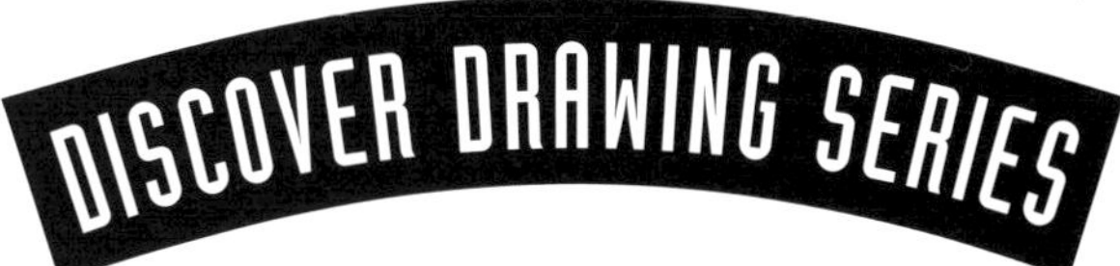

Draw Horses

Lee Hammond

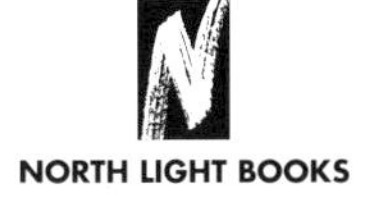

NORTH LIGHT BOOKS
Cincinnati, Ohio
www.artistsnetwork.com

ABOUT THE AUTHOR

Polly "Lee" Hammond is an illustrator and art instructor from the Kansas City area. She owns and operates the Midwest School of Illustration and Fine Art, Inc., where she teaches realistic drawing and painting.

She was raised and educated in Lincoln, Nebraska, and built her career in illustration and teaching in Kansas City. Although she has lived all over the country, she will always consider Kansas City home.

Lee resides in Overland Park, Kansas, along with her family.

Lee has been an author with North Light books since 1994. She also writes and illustrates articles for other publications such as *Artist's Magazine*. Lee is continuing to develop new art instruction books for North Light. She is expanding her career into children's books, which she will also illustrate. Fine art and limited edition prints of her work will soon be offered.

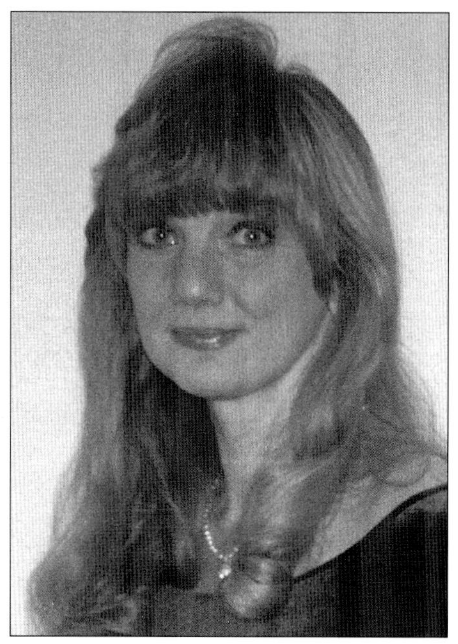

Note: You may contact Lee via e-mail at: Pollylee@aol.com.

 Published by North Light Books, an imprint of F+W Publications, Inc., 4700 East Galbraith Road, Cincinnati, Ohio, 45236. First edition.

Other fine North Light Books are available from your local bookstore or direct from the publisher.

10 09 11 10 9

Library of Congress Cataloging-in-Publication Data

Hammond, Lee.
Draw Horses / by Lee Hammond
p. cm.
Includes index.
ISBN-13: 978-1-58180-150-7 (pbk. : alk. paper)
ISBN-10: 1-58180-150-5 (pbk. : alk. paper)
1. Horses in art. 2. Drawing—Technique. I. Title.
NC783.8.H65 H36 2001 99-13009
743.6'96655—dc21 00-068112

Edited by Michael Berger and Elizabeth Sullivan
Interior production by Ben Rucker
Production coordinated by Mark Griffin

fw
F+W PUBLICATIONS, INC.

Metric Conversion Chart

to convert	to	multiply by
Inches	Centimeters	2.54
Centimeters	Inches	0.4
Feet	Centimeters	30.5
Centimeters	Feet	0.03
Yards	Meters	0.9
Meters	Yards	1.1
Sq. Inches	Sq. Centimeters	6.45
Sq. Centimeters	Sq. Inches	0.16
Sq. Feet	Sq. Meters	0.09
Sq. Meters	Sq. Feet	10.8
Sq. Yards	Sq. Meters	0.8
Sq. Meters	Sq. Yards	1.2
Pounds	Kilograms	0.45
Kilograms	Pounds	2.2
Ounces	Grams	28.4
Grams	Ounces	0.04

DEDICATION

This book is dedicated to Laura Tiedt. No words can possibly express the amount of unconditional love and support she has given me throughout the years. Her unending patience and understanding truly defines what genuine friendship is all about. Nothing I have done or accomplished over the last eight years would have been possible without her guiding light shining in my life. Thank you Laura, from the bottom of my heart!

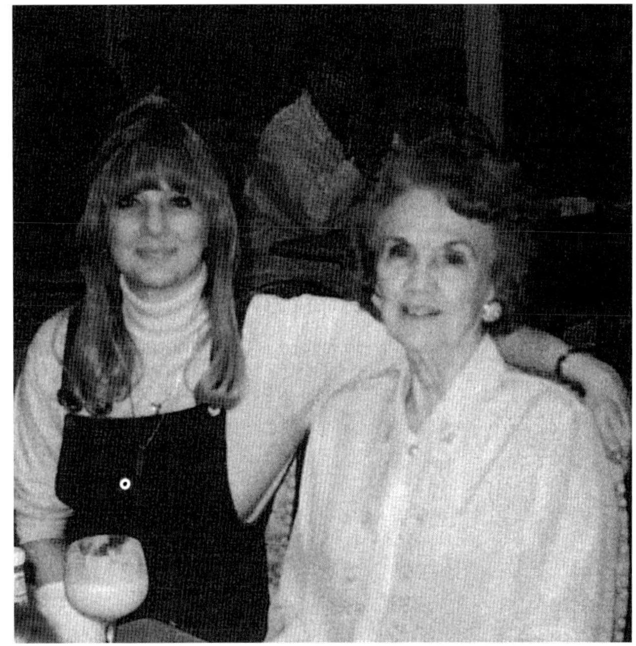

I also want to dedicate this to my mom, Dorothy Hagen. Everything I do, I do with you in my heart.

ACKNOWLEDGMENTS

Working on this book was a joy for me. All through my childhood my mother shared with me her love of horses. I remember every year for her birthday going in search of the perfect horse figurine to add to her collection. To this day, her hutch is filled with all of them, many dating back to before I was even born.

I also remember her stories. She had a horse named Cindy before she was married, and she shared with us the memories of riding Cindy. It was those stories that gave me a love of riding when I was young. Riding horses every summer at my friend Bob's stable became a regular routine, until long after I grew to be an adult.

Drawing the horses in this book gave me an opportunity to reflect on my fondest memories. It is for that reason I want to sincerely thank Greg Albert for allowing me the opportunity to once again write for North Light Books. I cannot imagine doing anything more enjoyable.

TABLE OF CONTENTS

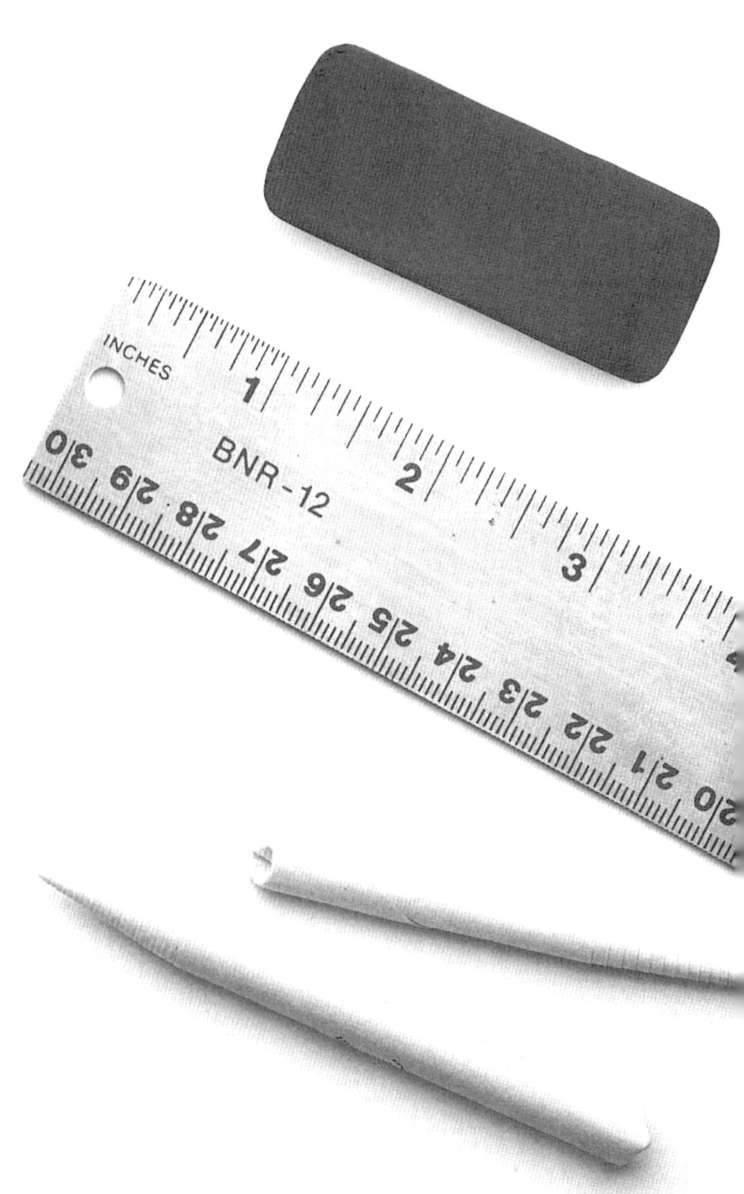
INCHES
BNR-12

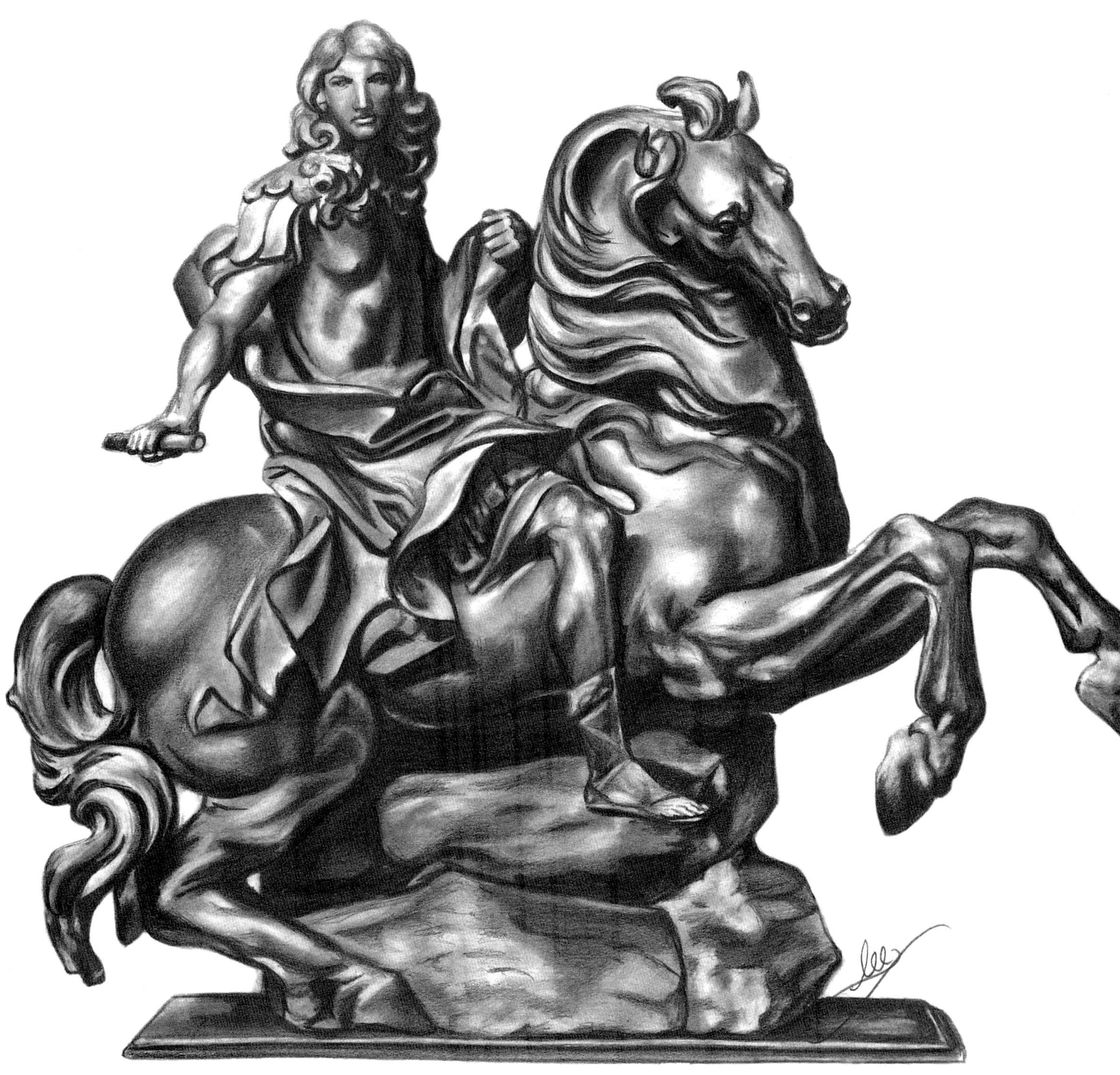

Copy of Model for Equestrian Statue of Louis XIV
By Gianlorenzo Bernini, 1670
11" × 14" (28cm × 36cm)
Graphite on smooth 2-ply Bristol

Chapter One

You Can Do It!

Nothing in this world has a shape as universally recognizable as the horse. Its shape has been the foundation for more art, architecture and designs than any other shape in history. From the earliest recorded drawings, dating back to the caveman era, the illustration of the horse proves that it has been a constant, useful companion to the human race.

Artists have incorporated the figure of the horse into their drawings, paintings and sculptures for centuries. The horse's smooth contours, delicate but strong features and graceful movements have made it one of the most popular subjects for art since the beginning of time.

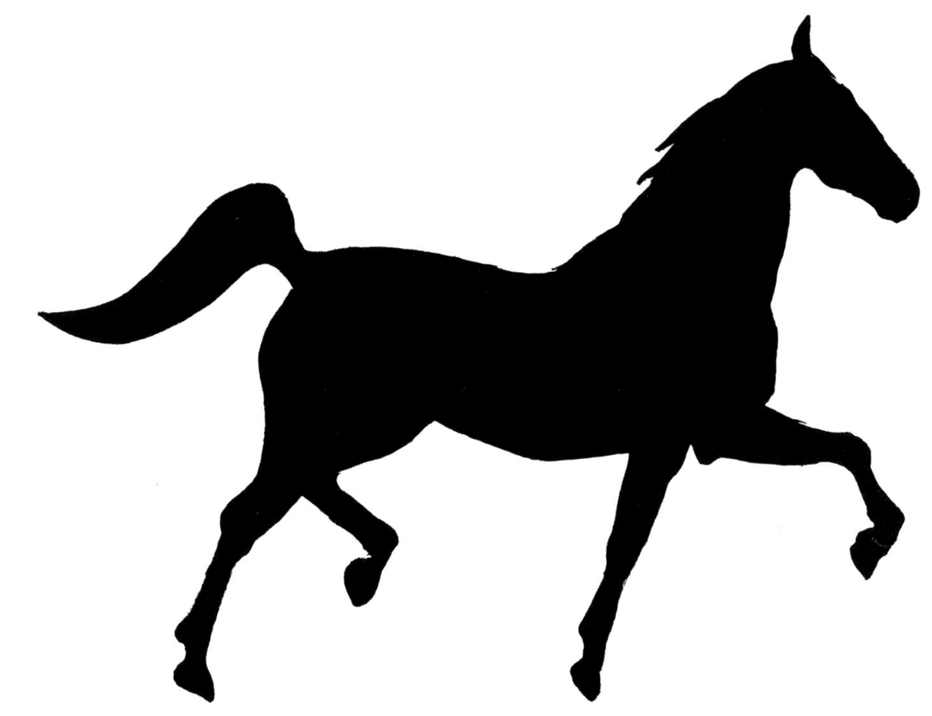

Silhouette of a horse.

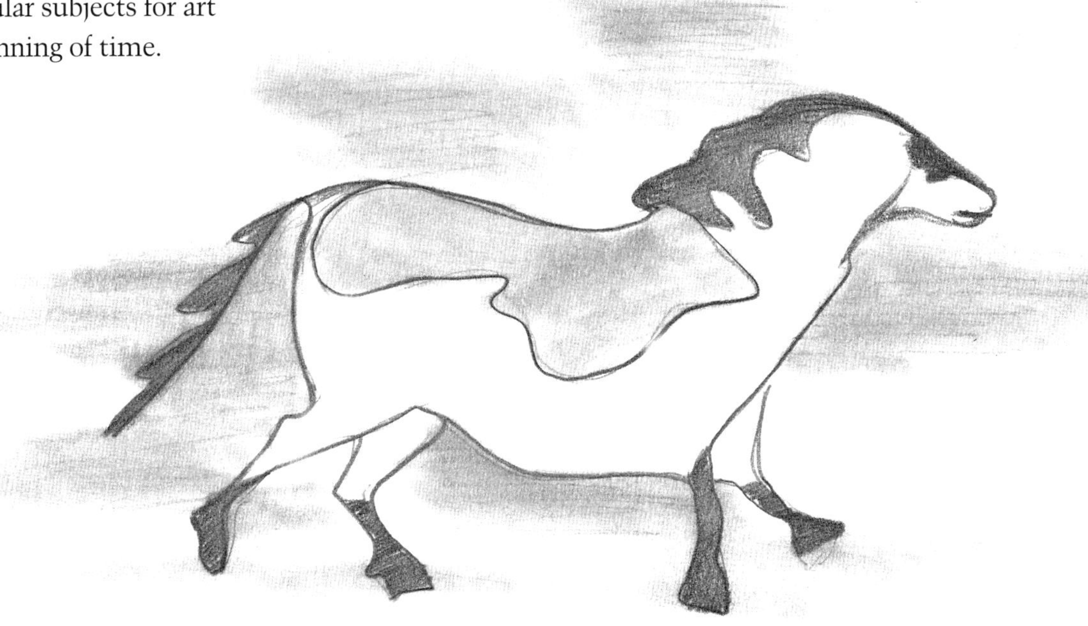

This replica of a typical cave drawing shows similarities to the horses of today, and how even primitive artists from ancient times had a fascination with their shape.

BEFORE AND AFTER

As children, we love to draw horses. After drawing people, it always seems to be one of the first complex subjects to be explored. As kids, we use our art as a means of expression, depicting our perceptions of life. Because they are more pictorial rather than finished art, children's drawings are simplistic, and reduced to mere lines and overall shapes. They are designed to tell us more of "what they are" than how they accurately appear.

You too, can create beautiful art if you follow the step-by-step instructions in this book. It has been written in such a manner that if you take it one chapter at a time and do the projects in the order that they are presented, drawing horses will become much easier for you. Practice is essential, but it will be worth it!

Drawing by Caroline Nyman, age 11.
I asked a young student of mine to look at a picture of a horse's face, and draw it for me. I asked her not to put in too much detail, but draw it using a typical sketching approach. This example is very typical of what most eleven-year-olds would do.

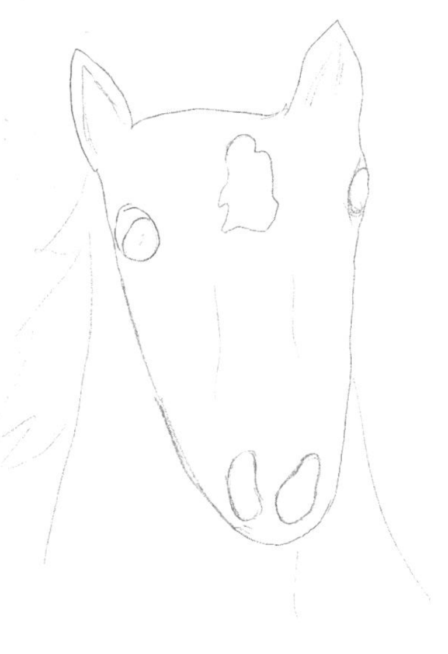

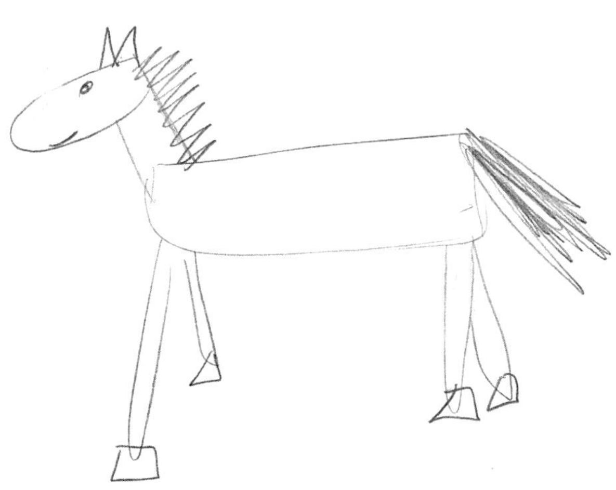

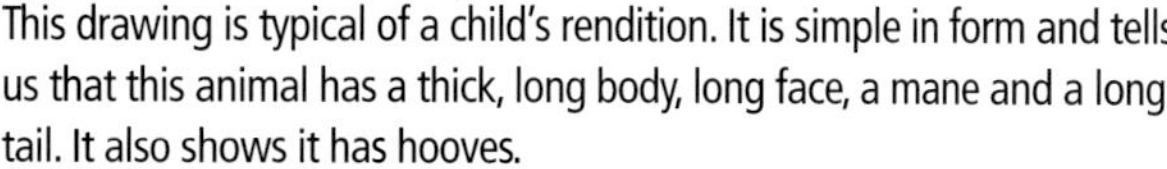

This drawing is typical of a child's rendition. It is simple in form and tells us that this animal has a thick, long body, long face, a mane and a long tail. It also shows it has hooves.

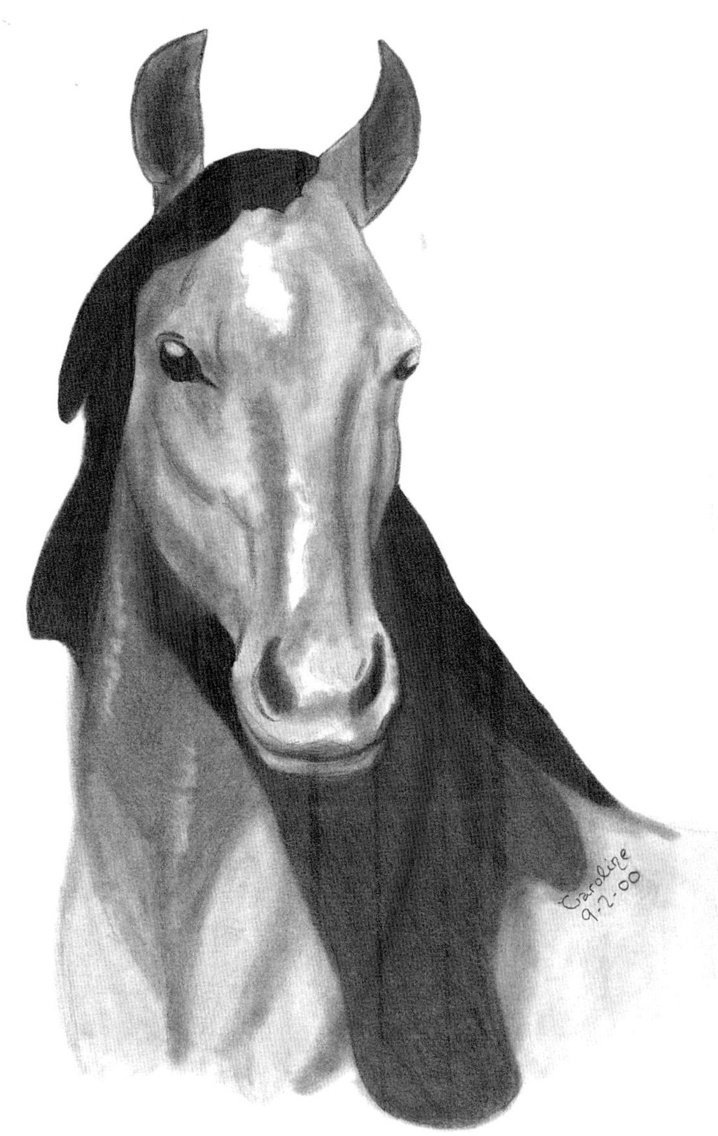

Drawing by Caroline Nyman, age 11.
The same student did this drawing. First, I showed her what to look for in capturing shapes. She then applied blending and shading to make it look more realistic.

This looks very advanced for someone of her age and proves what can be accomplished with a little guidance.

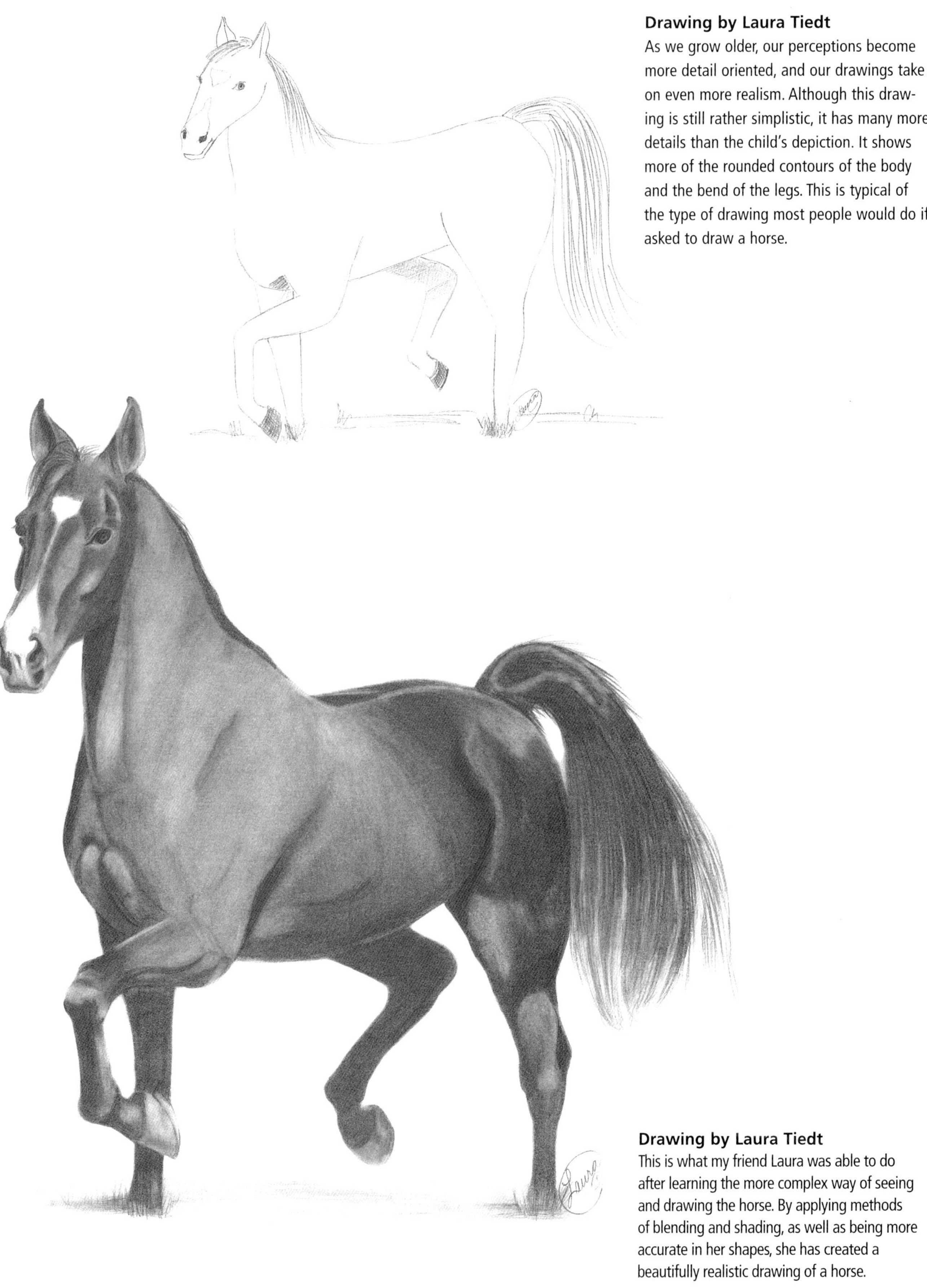

Drawing by Laura Tiedt
As we grow older, our perceptions become more detail oriented, and our drawings take on even more realism. Although this drawing is still rather simplistic, it has many more details than the child's depiction. It shows more of the rounded contours of the body and the bend of the legs. This is typical of the type of drawing most people would do if asked to draw a horse.

Drawing by Laura Tiedt
This is what my friend Laura was able to do after learning the more complex way of seeing and drawing the horse. By applying methods of blending and shading, as well as being more accurate in her shapes, she has created a beautifully realistic drawing of a horse.

Chapter Two

Materials

You cannot do quality artwork with inadequate art materials. My blended pencil technique requires the right tools to create the look. Do not scrimp in this department or your artwork will suffer. I have seen many of my students blame themselves for being untalented when it was their supplies keeping them from doing a good job. The following tools will help you be a better artist.

Smooth Bristol Boards or Sheets—Two-Ply or Heavier

This paper is very smooth (plate finish) and can withstand the rubbing associated with the technique I'll be showing you.

5mm Mechanical Pencil With 2B Lead

The brand of pencil you buy is not important; however, they all come with HB lead—you'll need to replace it with 2B lead.

Blending Tortillions

These are spiral-wound cones of paper. They are not the same as the harder, pencil-shaped stumps that are pointed at both ends. These are better suited for the blended pencil technique. Buy both large and small.

Kneaded Eraser

These erasers resemble modeling clay and are essential to blended pencil drawing. They gently "lift" highlights without ruining the surface of the paper.

Typewriter Eraser With a Brush on the End

These pencil-type erasers are handy due to the pointed tip, which can be sharpened. They are good for cleaning up edges and erasing stubborn marks, but their abrasive nature can rough up your paper.

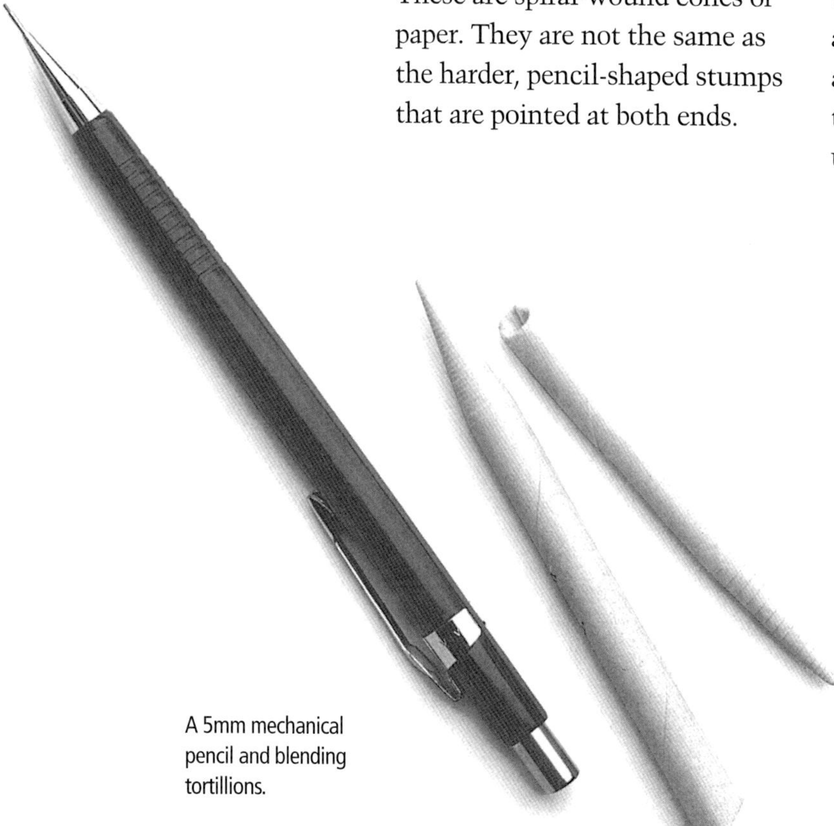

A 5mm mechanical pencil and blending tortillions.

Horsehair Drafting Brush

These wonderful brushes will keep you from ruining your work by brushing away erasings with your hand and smearing your pencil work. They will also keep you from spitting on your work by blowing the erasings away.

Pink Pearl or Vinyl Eraser

These erasers are meant for erasing large areas and lines. They are soft and nonabrasive and will not damage your paper.

Workable Spray Fixative

This is used to seal and protect your finished artwork. It's also used to fix an area of your drawing so it can be darkened by building up layers of tone. "Workable" means you can still draw on an arca after it has been sprayed.

Drawing Board

It's important to tilt your work toward you as you draw to prevent distortion that occurs when working flat. A board with a clip to secure your paper and reference photo will work best.

Ruler

This is used for graphing and measuring.

Acetate Report Covers

These are used for making graphed overlays to place over your photo references. They help you grid for accuracy what you are drawing.

Magazines

These are a valuable source of practice material. Collect magazine pictures and categorize them into files for quick reference.

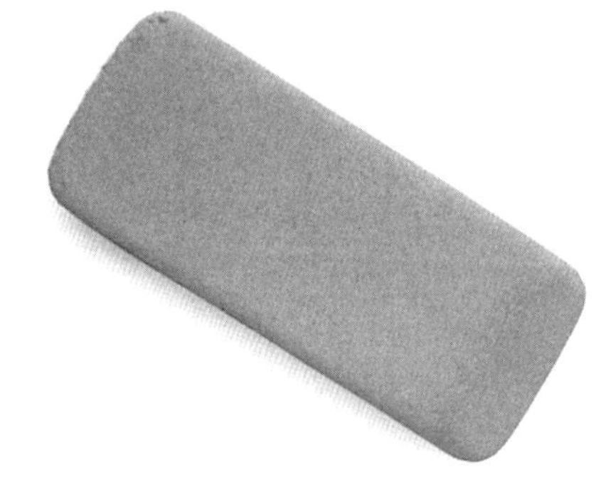

A typewriter eraser and Pink Pearl vinyl eraser.

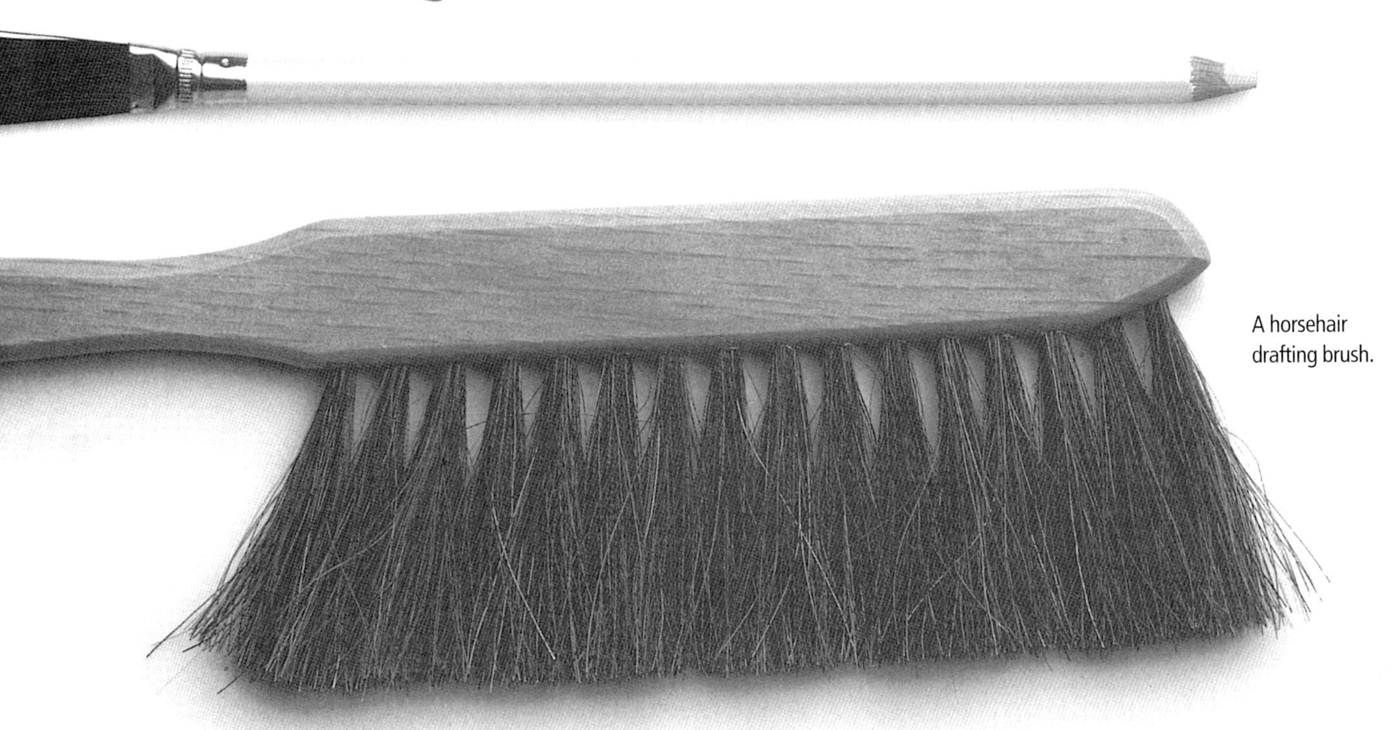

A horsehair drafting brush.

Chapter Three

Blending and Shading

The key to realistic drawing is not only in the accuracy of the shapes, but the illusion of form and dimension given to the drawing through the use of shading. Every object is affected by the elements of light and its surrounding shadows. If you can train yourself to see the effects of light on your subject matter, and replicate that look in your art, your work will take on a much more realistic impression.

We saw in the previous chapter how you can use outlines to create drawings. Although this method will indeed get your point across on the paper, it will not give you a realistic look. Anything drawn with an outlined approach will appear flat, empty and more like a cartoon.

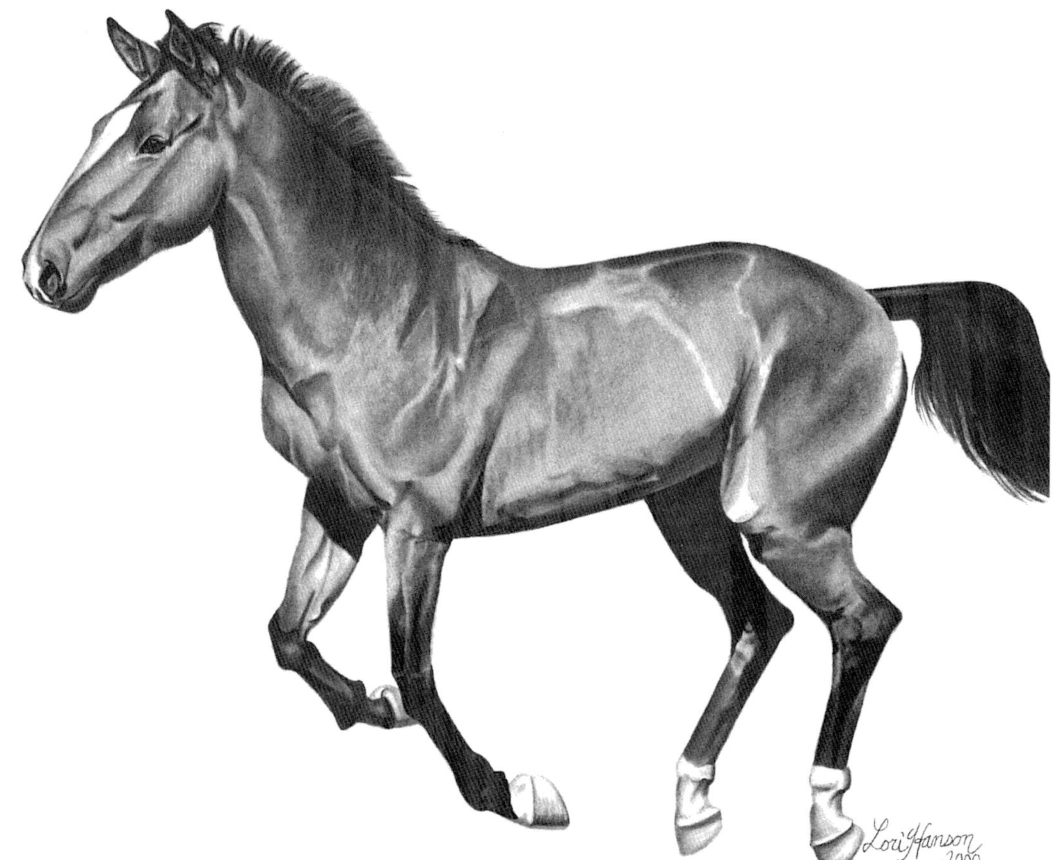

This student took a line drawing and applied the blending and shading methods to her work. The result is a very realistic drawing that accurately describes the smooth, shiny contours of a horse's body. The highlights and shadows give the drawing a lot of nice contrast, making it look very realistic. It is hard to believe that this was drawn by a 14-year-old.

Drawing of a Horse
11" × 14"
(28 cm × 36 cm)
Graphite on smooth 2-ply Bristol
Artist:
Lori Hanson, age 14

THE FIVE ELEMENTS OF SHADING

To draw realistically, you must fully understand how lighting affects an object. There are five elements of shading, shown in the box scale to the right, that are essential to realistically depicting an object's form. With any of these elements missing, your work will appear flat. Look at the sphere pictured here, and observe all the elements of shading.

1. Cast Shadow

The first box represents black and is the darkest tone found on your drawing. It is always opposite the light source. In the case of the sphere, it is found underneath. This area is void of light because, as the sphere protrudes, it blocks light and casts shadows.

2. Shadow Edge

The second box represents the dark gray and can be found in the area called the shadow edge. This area is where the sphere is turning back away from you and can be seen parallel to the edge.

3. Halftone

The third box represents a mid-gray or halftone. It is the area of the sphere that is not affected by either direct light or shadows.

4. Reflected Light

The fourth box represents a light gray, which can be seen in the reflected light area. Reflected light is always found along the edge of an object, and separates the darkness of the shadow edge from the darkness of the cast shadow.

5. Full Light

The fifth box represents white, and is the full light area where the light source is hitting the sphere at its strongest point.

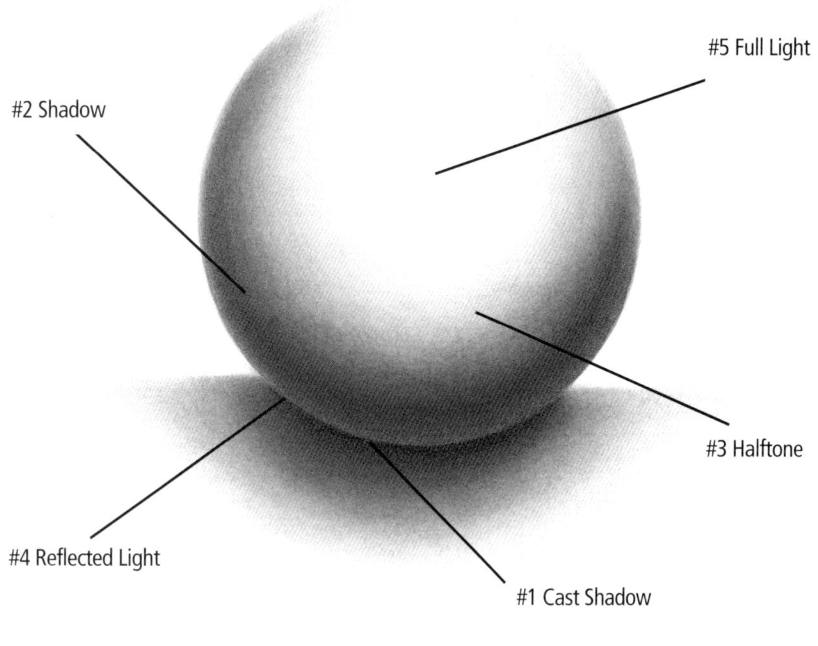

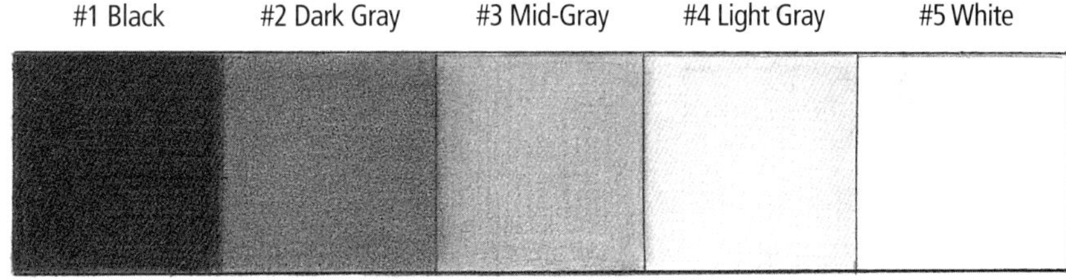

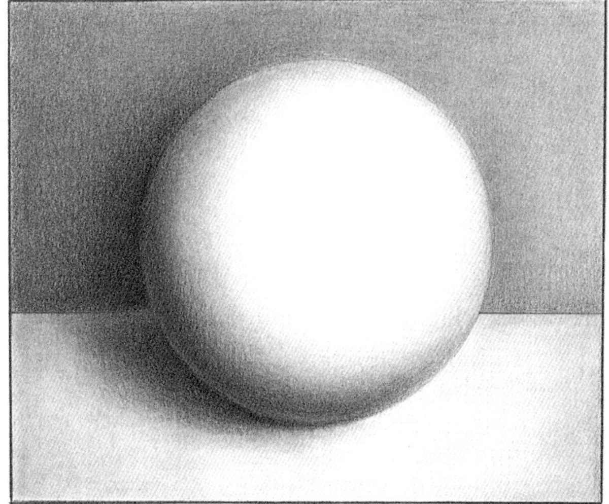

In order to show a light edge of a horse, you need a dark background. To show this technique, I created this sphere. The darker background makes the entire drawing seem less intense. The tones of the sphere seem subtler in contrast. Notice how there is no discernable outline around the sphere. All you see is tone against tone, which creates the edges.

BLENDING

To create smooth blending, you must first learn to use your tools and apply the pencil lines properly. If the pencil lines have been applied rough and uneven, no amount of blending later will smooth them out. Take a look at the examples below. The top sample shows poor pencil application. Notice how the scribbled lines look sloppy.

In the sample below, see how the lines have been applied so close together you cannot see white areas between them? This is very important. By applying the lines closely, and in an up-and-down fashion, the pencil lines fill in. Keep adding tone until you build up a deep black, and then lighten your touch and gradually get lighter as you go to the right. By going back and forth, overlapping your tones, you will make it look gradual. You do *not* want to see where one tone ends, and the next begins.

When you have finished applying the pencil, blend your value scale out with a tortillion. Use the same up-and-down, back-and-forth motion you used with your pencil. Lighten your touch as you proceed to the right, and gently blend the light area into the white of the paper until you can no longer tell where it ends. If choppiness appears in your blending, there are some tricks to correcting them. First, squint your eyes. This helps blur your vision and allows you to see the imperfections by making the tones seem more intense. The dark areas will appear darker, and the light areas lighter.

Should you see any unwanted dark spots in the drawing, take a piece of your kneaded eraser and roll it between your thumb and forefinger to create a point. Gently lift the dark spot out by stroking it lightly. Never dab at it. This will make it uneven. This is not really erasing, but drawing in reverse. It is a controlled technique of adding light.

After you are done lifting dark spots, squint your eyes once again. Look for light areas that are too light. Gently fill them in with your pencil. Your value scale should now be smooth and gradual. Don't be discouraged if it doesn't come easy for you the first time. I make my students practice this over and over.

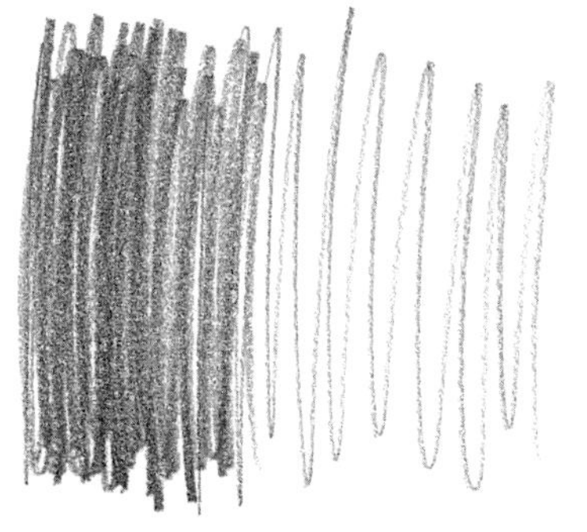

An incorrectly drawn value scale. The scribbled application of pencil lines makes this scale impossible to blend out evenly.

A blended value scale from dark to light. This scale is smooth and even in its tones.

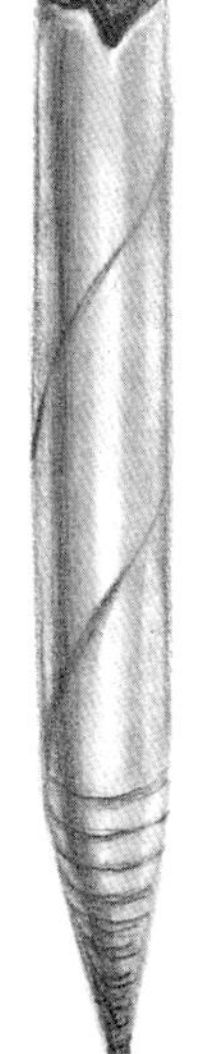

A tortillion is nothing more than paper wrapped into a cone shape. Never use the tortillion on its tip. This will cause it to collapse.

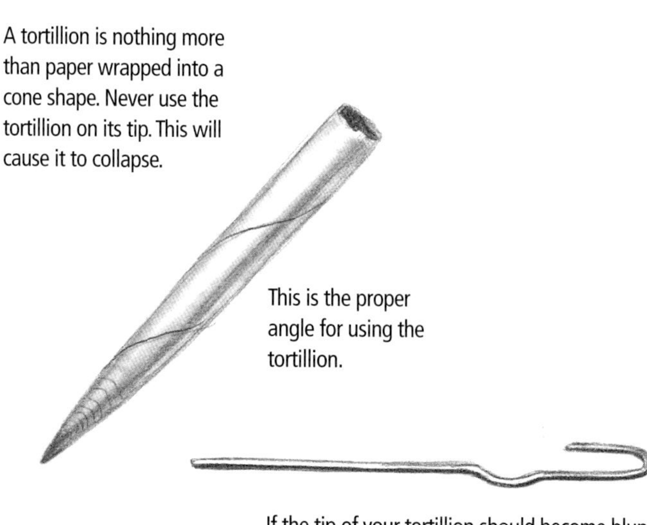

This is the proper angle for using the tortillion.

If the tip of your tortillion should become blunt, straighten out a large paper clip and gently stick it into the end to push the point back out.

BLENDING PROJECT

STEP 1: APPLY CAST SHADOWS

Begin drawing the sphere by first tracing a perfect circle. Apply the #1 tone (Black) to the Cast Shadow area below it. Can you see how this creates the illusion of a tabletop?

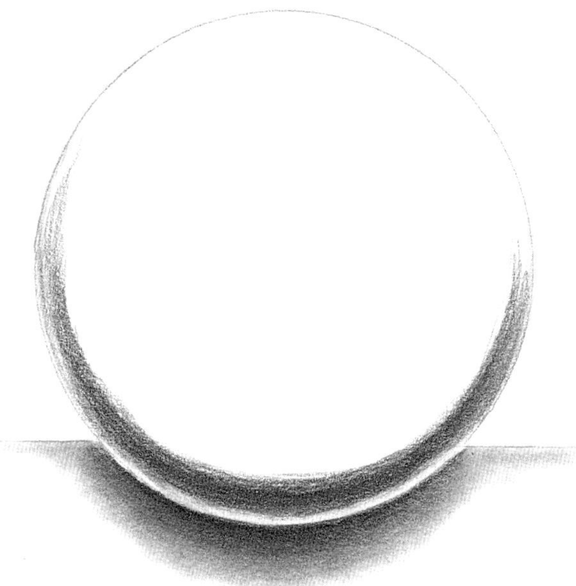

STEP 2: APPLY SHADOW EDGE

Apply the #2 tone (Dark Gray) to the Shadow Edge area. Be sure to parallel the edge of the circle.

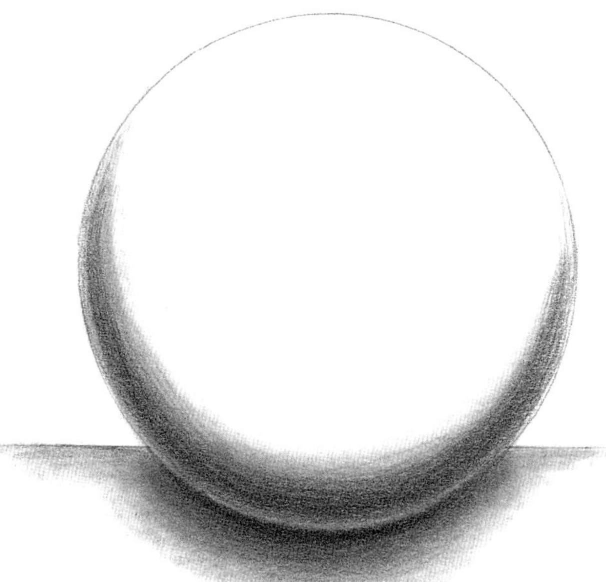

STEP 3: BLEND

Gently blend with the tortillion, going "with" the shape until it fades into the full light area of the sphere.

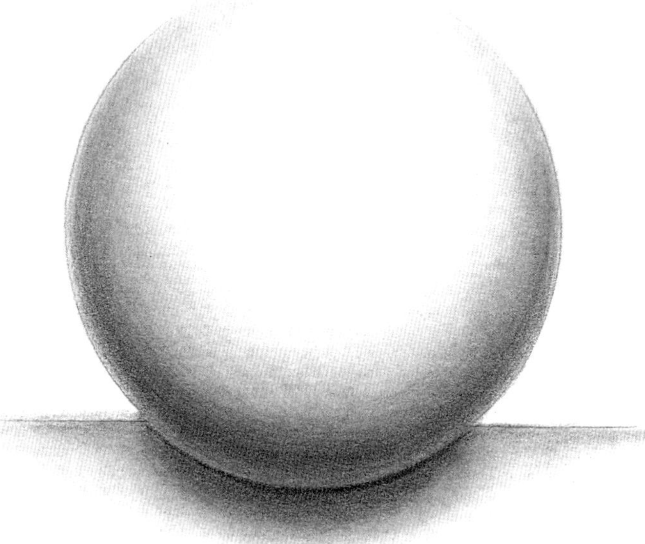

STEP 4: CORRECT IMPERFECTIONS

Squint your eyes and look at your drawing. If there are any imperfections in the blending, use the tricks of your tools to correct them. This is what a completed sphere should look like.

One of the most common problems I see when teaching is the resistance of the students to get dark with their tones. It is for that reason that I have signs all over the studio saying, "Get it Darker!!!!!" Once you are no longer hesitant to create deep tones, your work will appear more realistic.

Study the tones of this horse. Although it is extremely dark, there are subtle light areas of tone throughout the drawing. Look at the contours of the face. You can see the light along the edge of the cheek and in the raised surface of the veins. It is very hard to leave these areas light as you draw, so I find it easier to lift them out with a pointed piece of my kneaded eraser. The result is much more subtle and realistic looking. Remember, this is drawing in reverse. You are not erasing—you are drawing in light!

Although we will cover drawing hair later, I want you to look at the forelock. Can you see how I used the lifting technique to create the highlights in the hair? It is a wonderful way of creating the look of light.

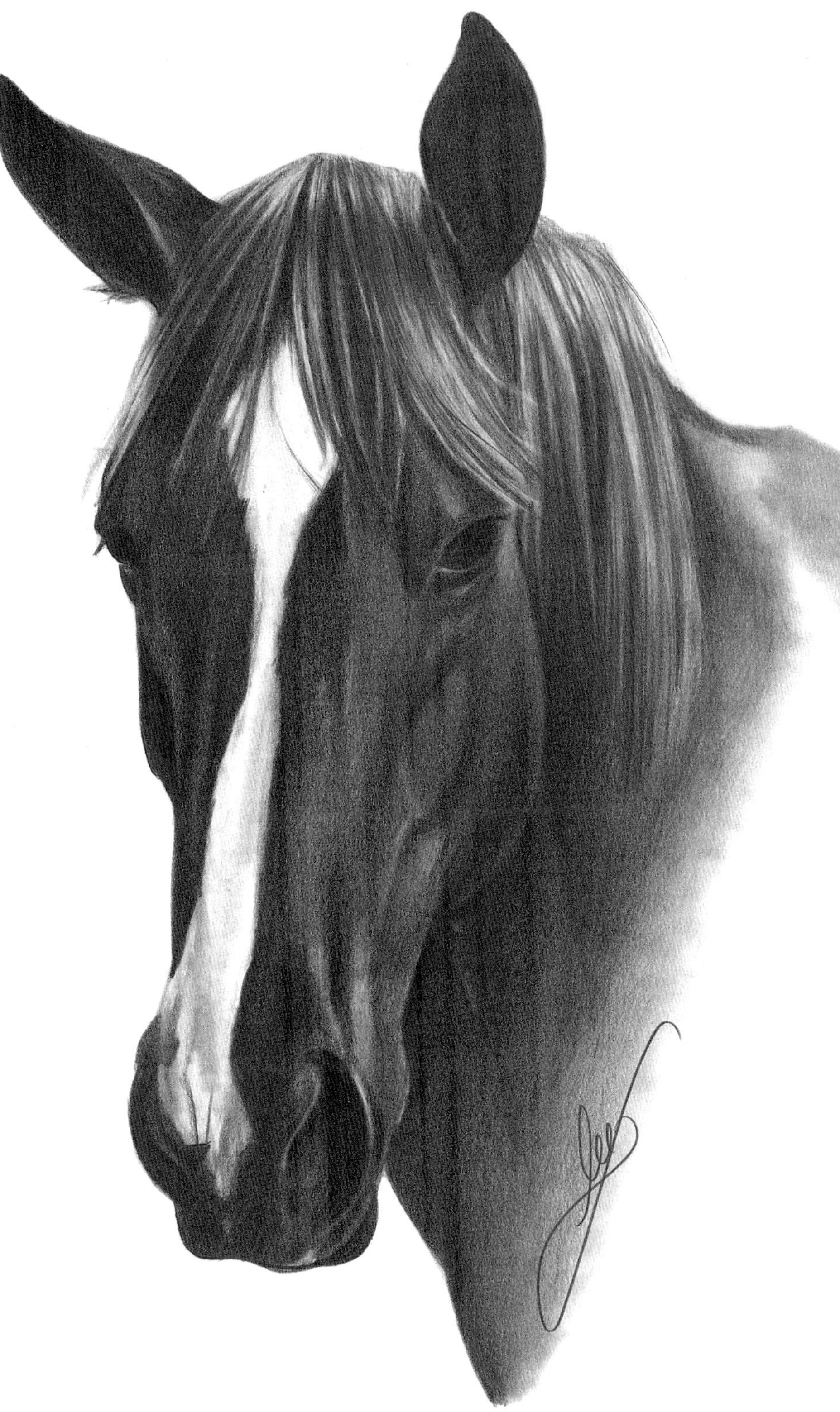

This drawing is a good example of drawing a dark horse on a white background. No background shading was necessary to help describe the edges. Notice how the dark tones create an edge, instead of using a hard outline around the shape of the horse. The result is a very realistic rendition.

When drawing something that is white, it is important to create the edge of the subject without the use of hard lines. This is one of the crucial keys to realism. As with the sphere exercise, a darker tone has been placed behind this white colored horse. This was done to avoid the use of outlining to separate the horse from the white of the paper. The result is a horse that looks very dimensional.

If you look closely at the drawing, you will see the sphere exercise repeated in the cheek area. Can you see the five elements of shading here? Look at all of the edges along the horse's face. You will see reflected light showing against the shaded background, except for the dark area of the upper lip. This is because in this area the edge is much darker than the background tones.

To create the subtle light areas of the face, I used the same lifting technique I applied to the dark horse on the previous page. Always remember to lift the light out instead of drawing around it. It looks more reflective and natural this way.

To create the background shading, I gently applied the tone with my pencil and used a dirty tortillion to smooth out the tones. Save your dirty tortillions for areas like these. Only throw them away if the tips become weak and bent.

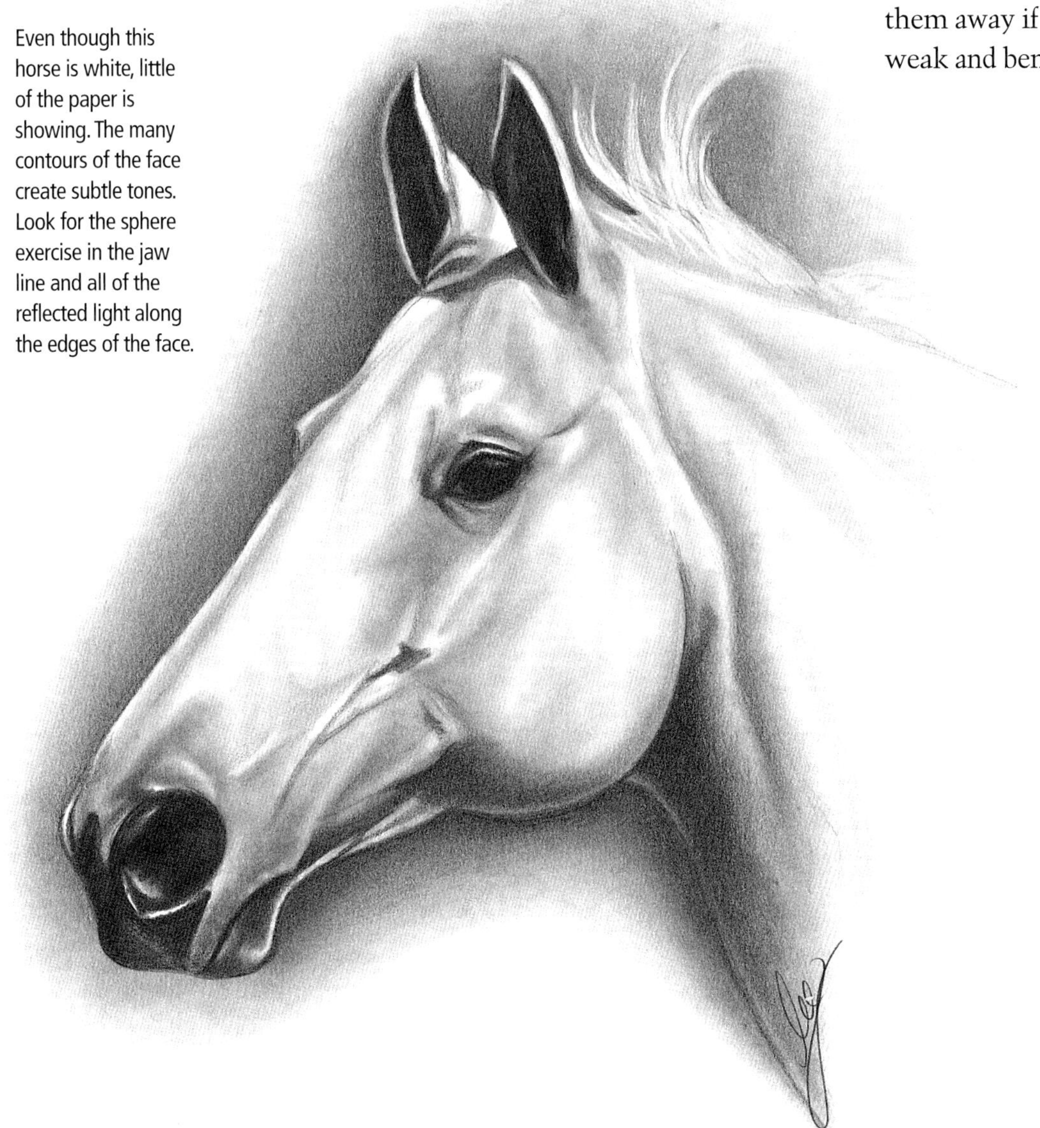

Even though this horse is white, little of the paper is showing. The many contours of the face create subtle tones. Look for the sphere exercise in the jaw line and all of the reflected light along the edges of the face.

Chapter Four

Graphing and Shapes

To apply the principles of blending and shading that we learned in the previous chapter, we must first have an accurate foundation to build on. It is essential to have your shapes accurate before you begin the blending phase, as it is very difficult to change or alter the shape once that amount of tone is in place.

When drawing, everything we look at should be viewed as a collection of interlocking shapes. One shape will lead to another. Try to not see the subject for what it is, but more for what it looks like.

By doing the puzzle exercise below, it will reinforce the fact that you can draw accurately. It is easy to draw shapes when they don't look like anything recognizable.

None of the shapes in these boxes resemble anything, so you will have no problem drawing them. It is only when we recognize something that it becomes difficult, because we will draw from memory instead of observation.

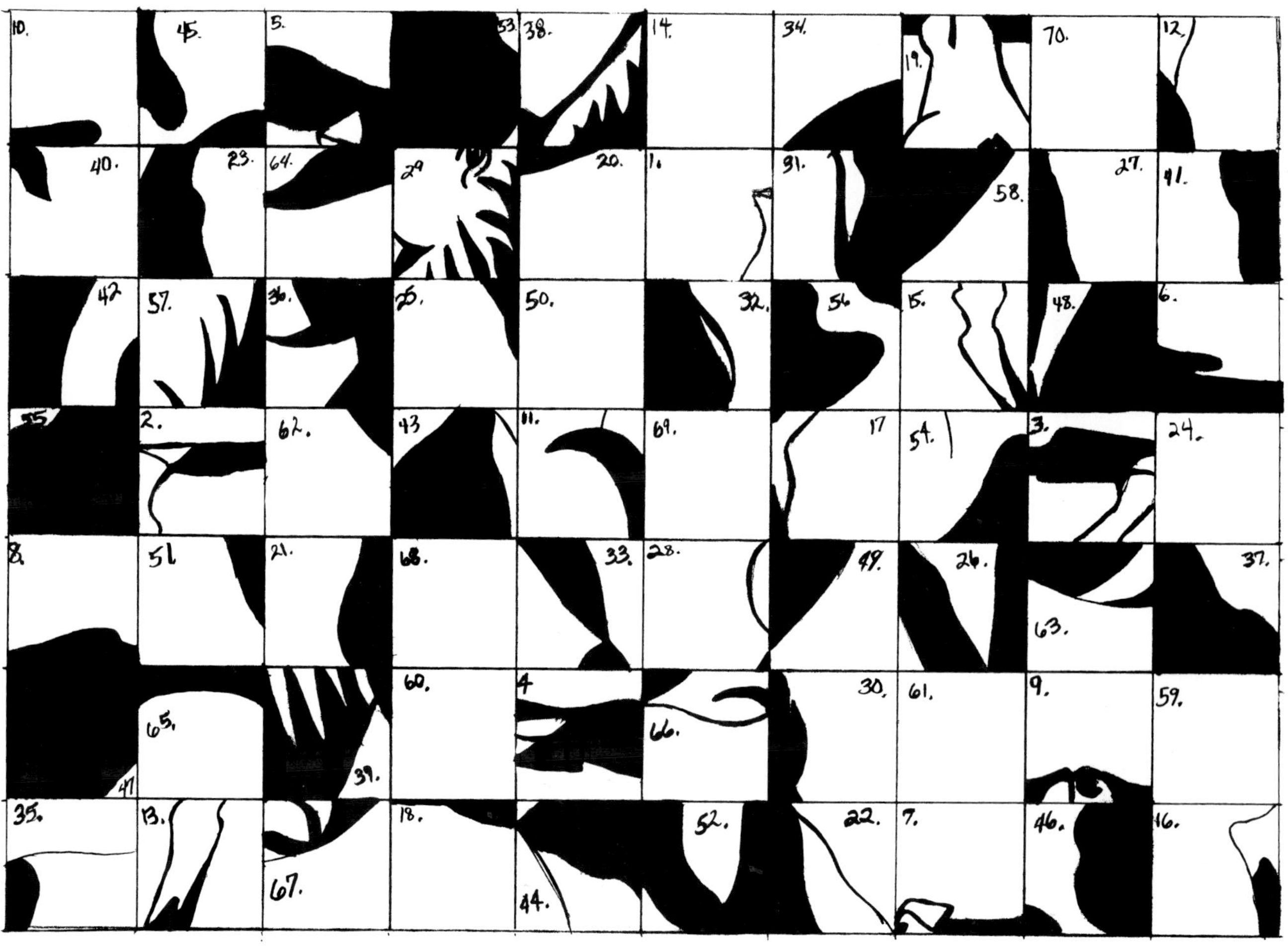

1	2	3	4	5	6	7	8	9	10
11	12	13	14	15	16	17	18	19	20
21	22	23	24	25	26	27	28	29	30
31	32	33	34	35	36	37	38	39	40
41	42	43	44	45	46	47	48	49	50
51	52	53	54	55	56	57	58	59	60
61	62	63	64	65	66	67	68	69	70

This puzzle exercise may seem a bit juvenile at first, but it is an excellent exercise to practice drawing shapes. Each one of these boxes in the illustration to the left has a number and a shape drawn in it. None of these shapes by themselves mean anything. In each box of the empty graph above, draw what you see, by placing the shapes in the corresponding numbered box. Do not try to figure out what it is you are drawing, because you will start drawing from memory without even knowing it. Just draw what you see as accurately as possible. When you are finished with this puzzle, turn your work upside down to see what it is.

GRAPHING EXERCISE

You can break down anything you see into the same type of puzzle by placing an acetate grid over a photograph. You can also have the photo copied, and draw your grid on that. By studying the shapes in each individual box, the image becomes more abstract. You can further your objectivity by turning the photo upside down, which will make it even more unrecognizable.

With your pencil and a ruler, very lightly draw a graph on your drawing paper. It is important to draw very lightly, as these lines will need to be erased later on. Use the same size squares as the grid you drew over the photo, which will make your drawing the same size. If you want to make the drawing a bit bigger, simply use larger squares on your drawing paper.

If you draw the shapes inside the boxes as accurately as possible, all of the lines will connect properly and create the desired shape. Be sure to get everything, including shadows and highlights—these areas should be viewed as shapes also.

When you are finished and you are sure that you have drawn as accurately as possible, gently and carefully remove your grid lines. Do not erase your line drawing! Be sure to save the drawing you create during this exercise for a demonstration later in the book.

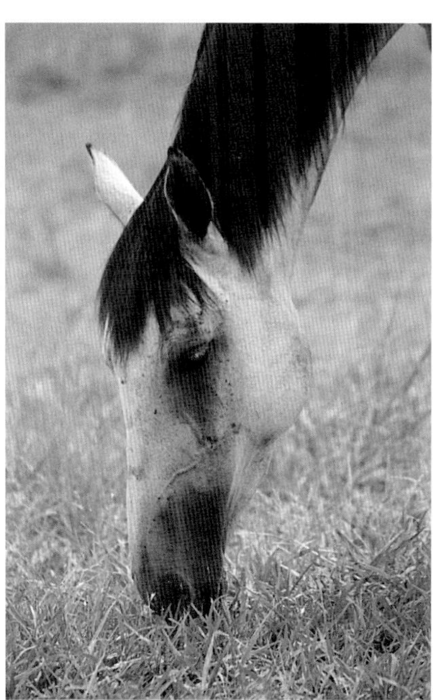

This is a beautiful photo of a horse. The size of the face and the lighting make it a perfect candidate for drawing.

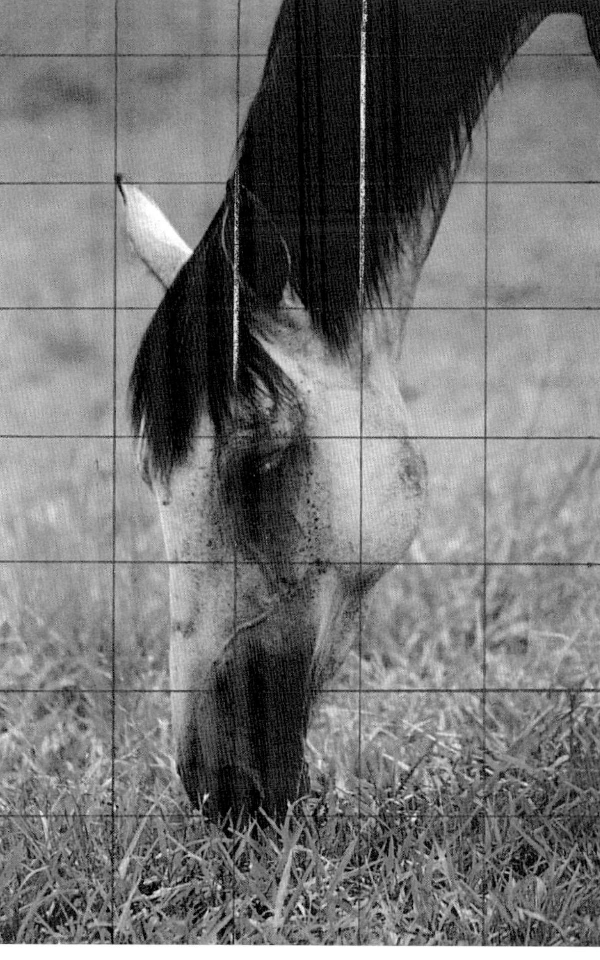

By placing a grid over the photo, you can create the same puzzle-like exercise as the one on the previous pages. Turn the photo upside down as you work to be sure you draw what you see, and not from what you remember.

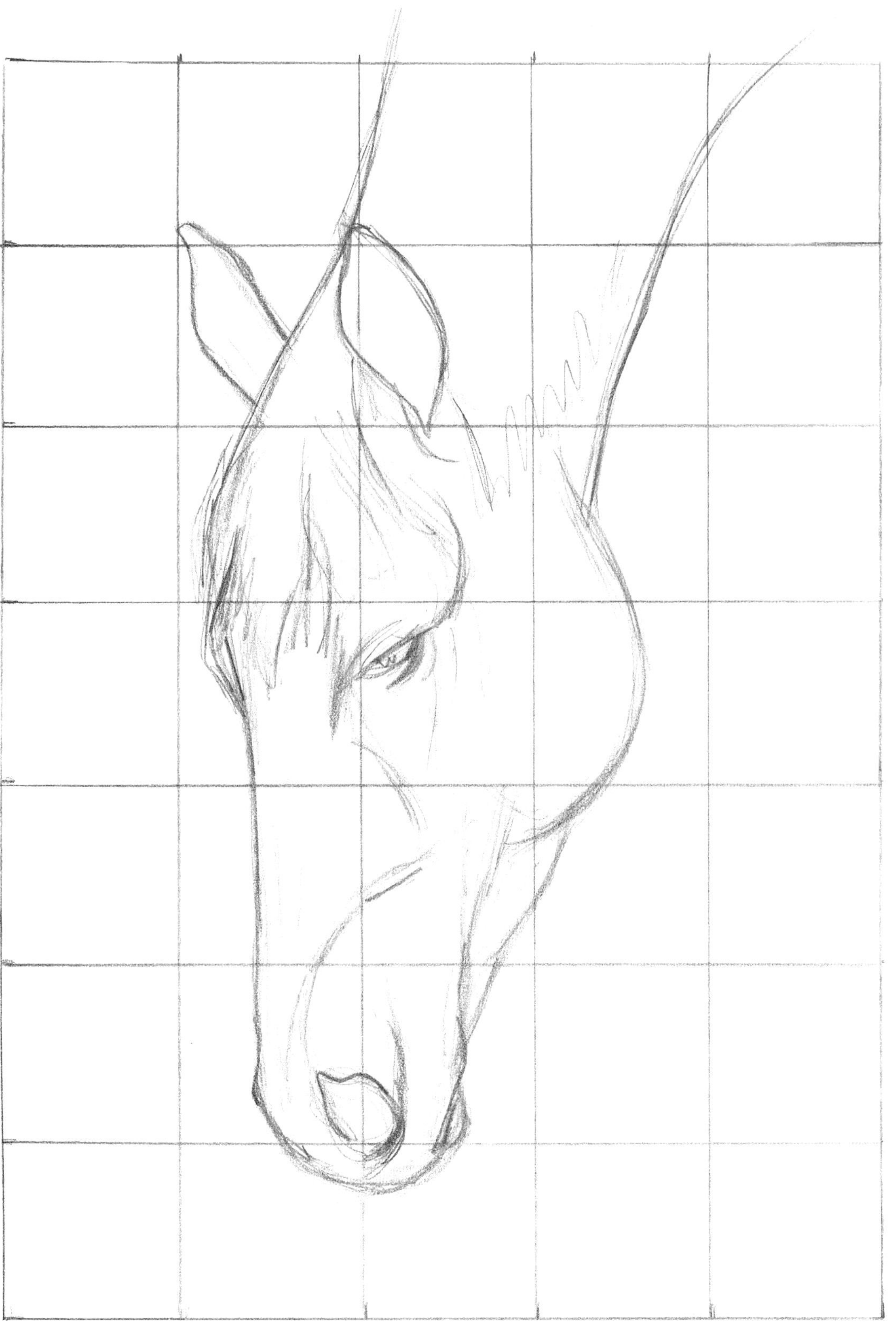

An accurate line drawing of the photograph.

Chapter Five

Horse Anatomy

To draw a horse accurately, it is helpful to know what makes the body look the way it does. By viewing the skeleton and seeing the bone structure, you can see how the shape of the horse is created. Look at the curves and angles of the bone formation; you can see these replicated in the horse's features.

Study various pictures of horses. Better yet, if you have access to real ones, closely observe them. Take photos for closer examination later. Look for all of the muscles and the shapes they create. Look for protruding surfaces that gather light and recessed areas that harbor shadows. Look for the five elements of shading in the forms that you see, and try to incorporate as much of these elements into your drawing as possible.

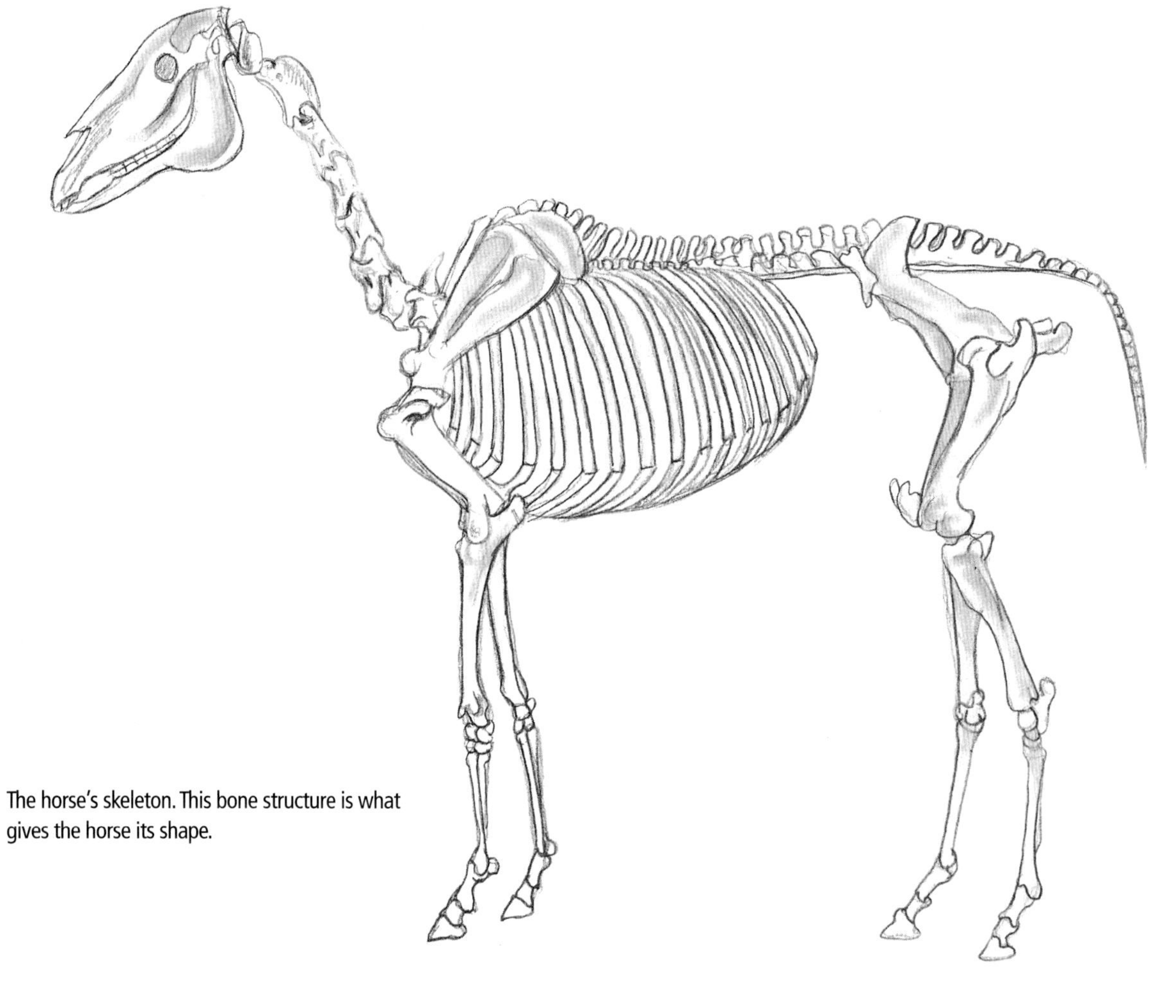

The horse's skeleton. This bone structure is what gives the horse its shape.

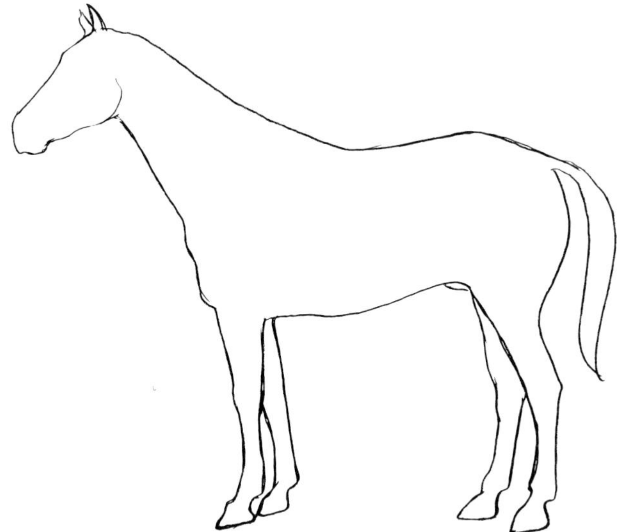

There is more to the horse than just bone. This line drawing shows how the muscles and flesh fill out the form, giving it a rounder appearance. Although this drawing resembles a horse, it is cartoonlike due to the lack of detail.

This realistic illustration of a horse shows the contours of the muscles. The light reflects off of the areas that bulge, and shadows can be seen where areas recede. This is a very muscular horse. Look at the chest area and you can see where the muscles divide down the middle. Look closely at the front legs and you can see the veins of the legs stretched over the muscle formation. It is this type of detail that can make the difference between an average drawing and an excellent illustration.

"Boston Charmer" World Champion Stallion, 1980
Photograph compliments of Barbara Aldridge

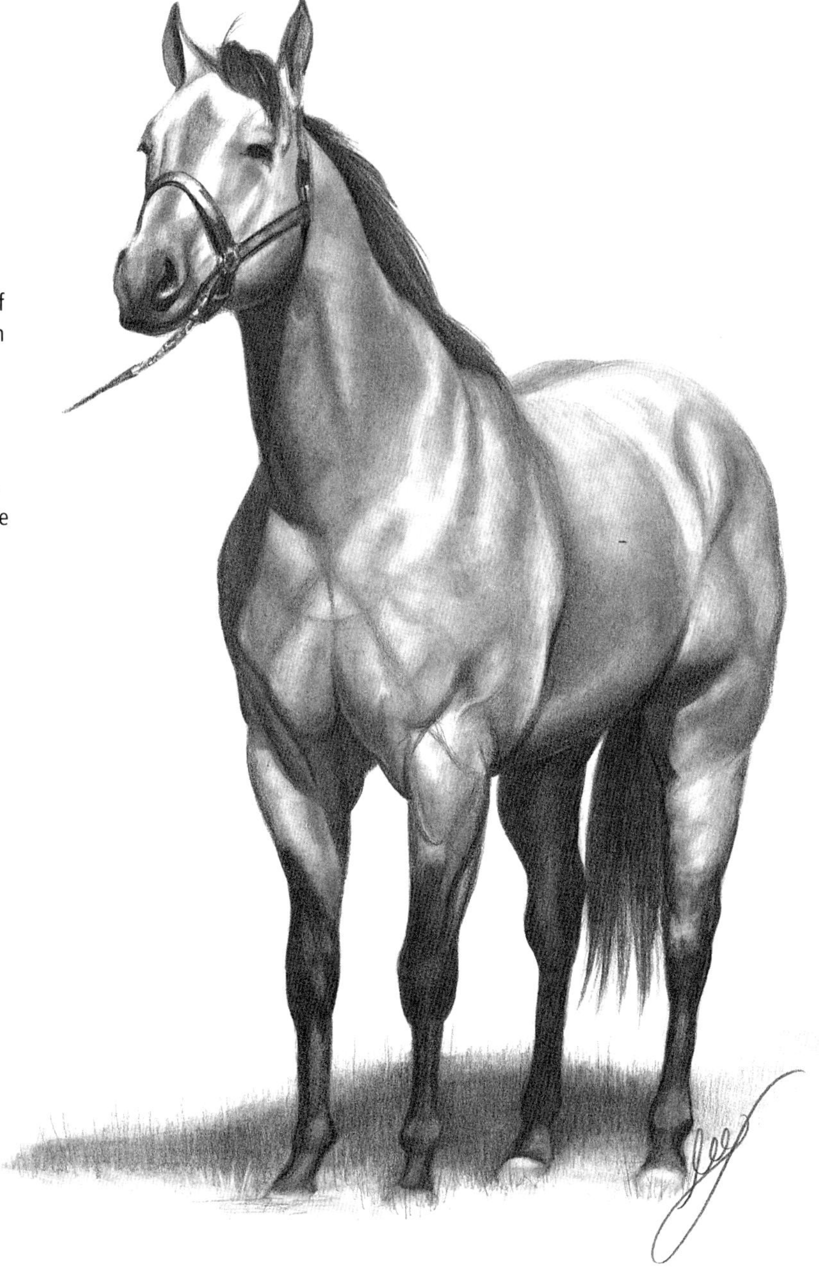

BASIC SHAPES

When you draw, try to see the basic shapes that make up the form. The following are a few of the basic shapes you will see when drawing horses. Draw these shapes for practice. Apply the blending technique to each of them, remembering the five elements of shading as you go. It will make drawing the horse easier.

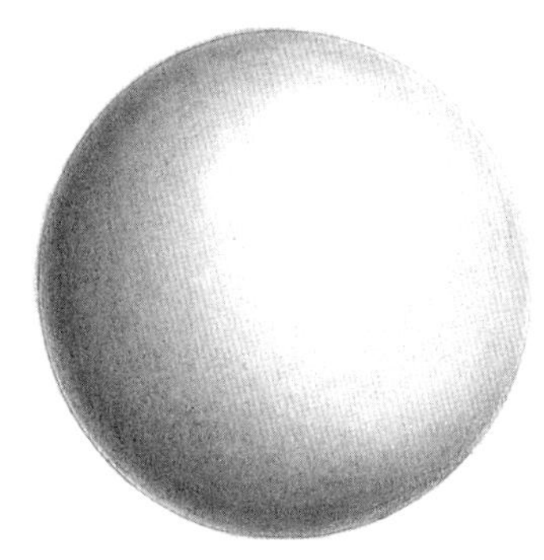

Sphere
This shape can be found in any rounded area.

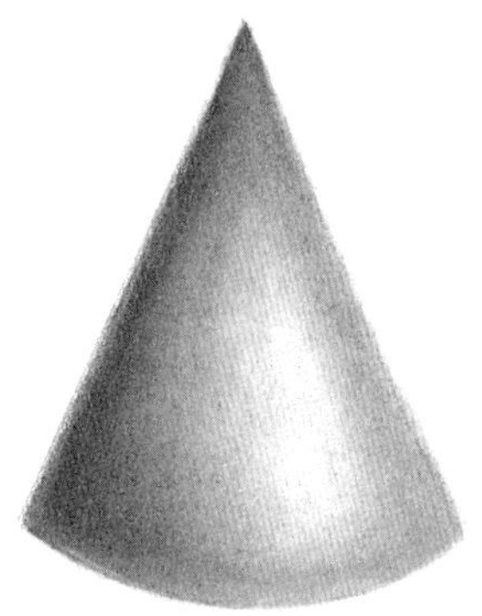

Cone
Look for this shape in the face and legs.

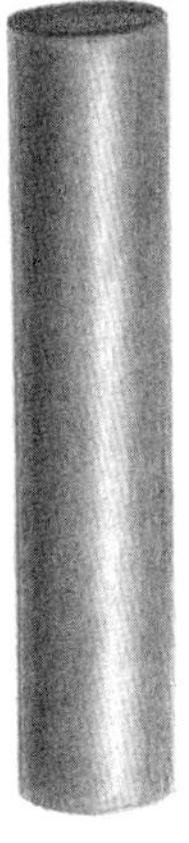

Elongated Cylinder
This is what makes up the shape of the legs.

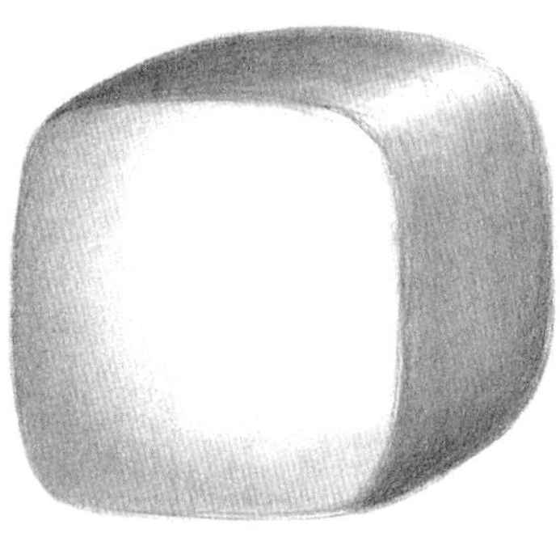

Cube
This can be found in areas such as the rump and belly.

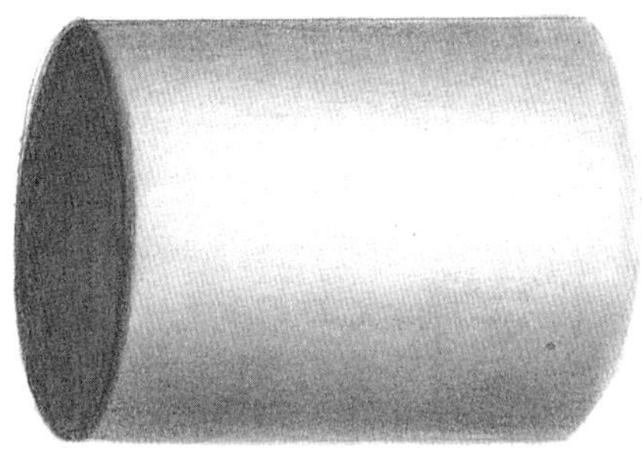

Heavy Cylinder
This can be used for the trunk and the neck shape.

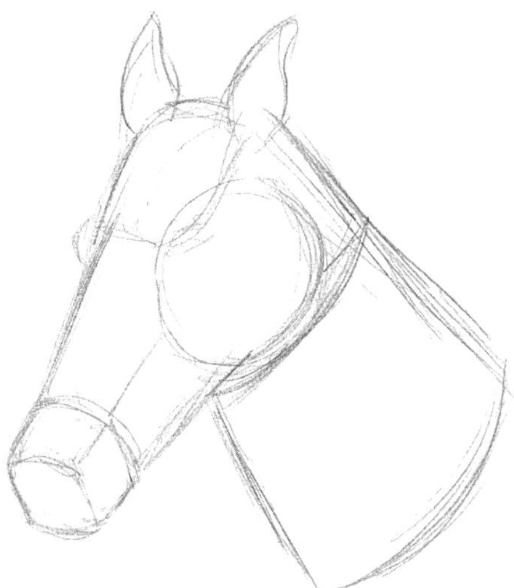

This horse head and neck are made up of a cone and cylinder. By seeing it in basic terms, you can see how angular the shapes really are, and avoid drawing things too round.

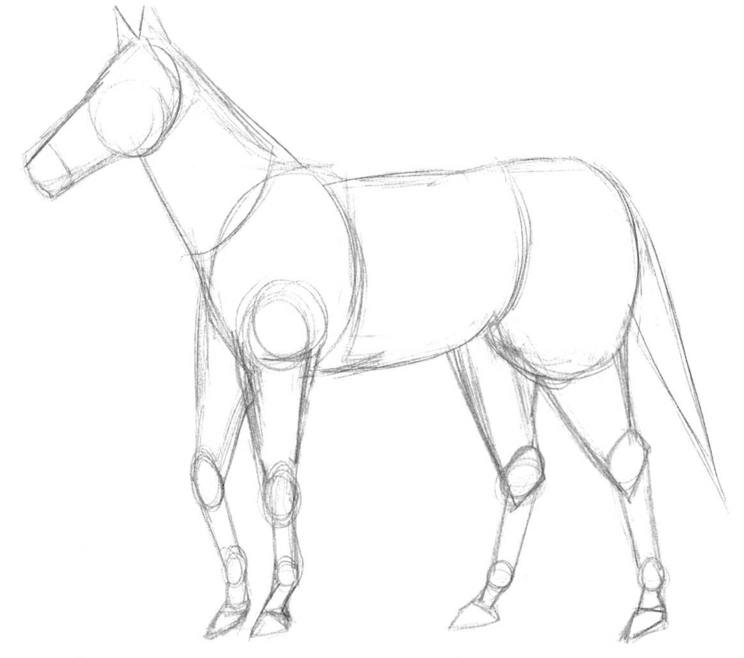

Look at all of the cylinders in this example. Again, be sure to look carefully for the many angles that make up the shapes. Notice how the legs are extremely angular, due to the joints.

Compare the two drawings on the top half of this page. Can you see how the application of basic shapes can help you see the angles in the form of the horse? Even some of the rounded shapes have slight angles to them.

Look at the area of the stomach and the rump. Can you see that it is really more angular and cube shaped than circular? The same is true for the knee and ankle joints. By adding a hint of angle to them, they will not appear too round.

The rear view of the horse, on the bottom half of this page shows the squared appearance of the rump. This is often drawn too round, giving the horse an unnatural curviness. The rump is more of a cube shape than a sphere. Try seeing the angular shapes in everything you draw. It will give your drawings more realism.

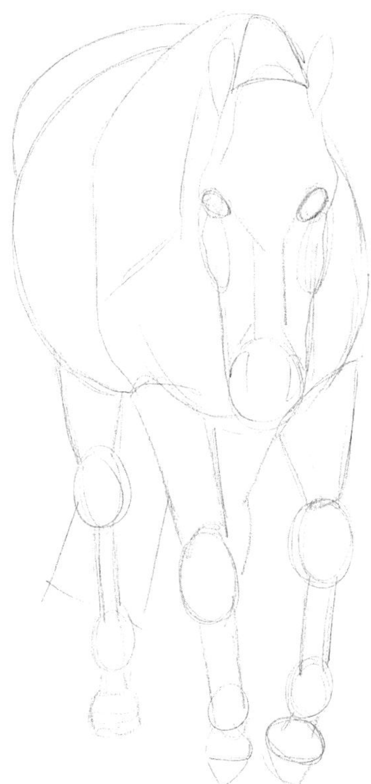

By drawing in the basic shapes, the overall shape of the horse is easier to see.

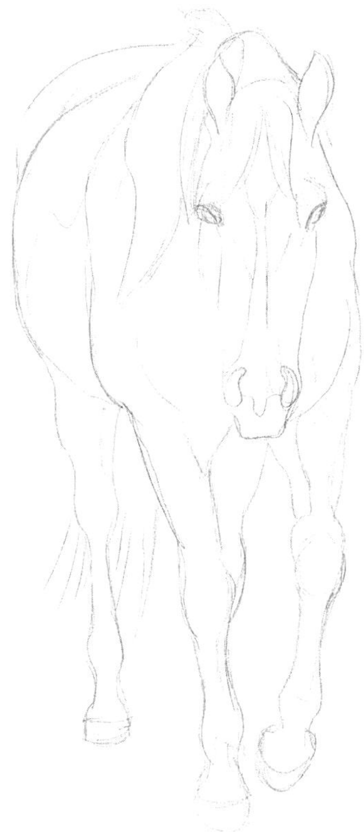

By gently rounding out some of the angles, the horse takes on a realistic, natural shape.

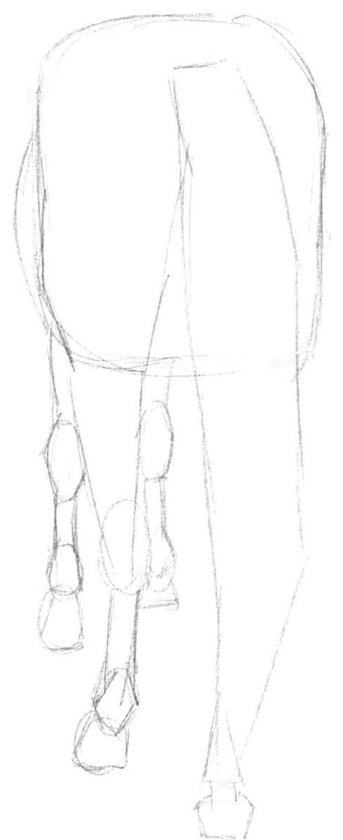

This view of the rear shows how squared off the rump really is. Don't draw this area too round.

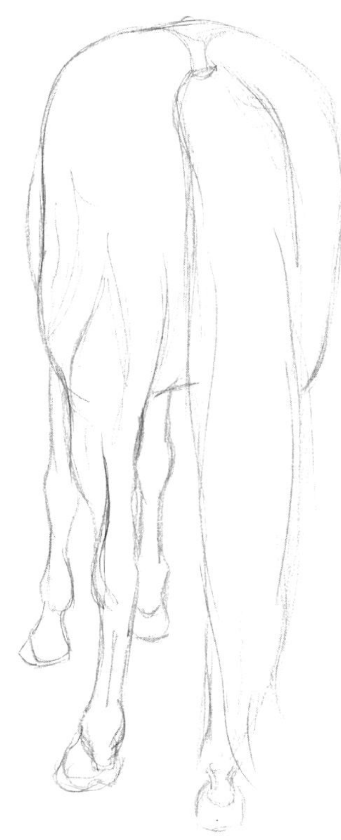

The rump gently curves, but still maintains the look of a cube, rather than a sphere.

Chapter Six

Horse Types

There are over 150 types and breeds of horses worldwide. Each has its own unique qualities and characteristics. As artists, the variances in the breeds are most interesting to us due to the way each one of them looks. The different breeds vary not only in their colors and markings, but also in their body structure. Some have thick muscular bodies and have been used by man for working and hauling. Some are more delicate in their build. Some are very small, while others appear massive. Some breeds are light in color, and others are dark. Some are a little bit of both. There are horses with stripes, and horses with spots. Each and every one of them is fun to draw.

Not all horses are created equal, and it would take forever to cover all of the different breeds. There are many wonderful books and magazines on the subject, full of great pictures to draw from. I suggest finding a good reference book to study as you are learning the techniques in this book. It will be good practice for you to draw as many as you can. Look for your own subjects to draw as well. Take your camera with you out in the country or to the local zoo, and have some fun taking your own reference pictures!

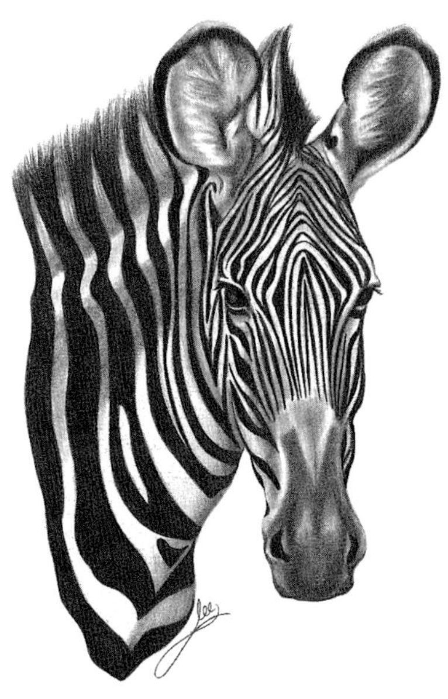

Many horses have unmistakable features. No horse is more readily recognized than the beautiful striped zebra. It has been the focus of many pieces of artwork and photography because of its incredible beauty.

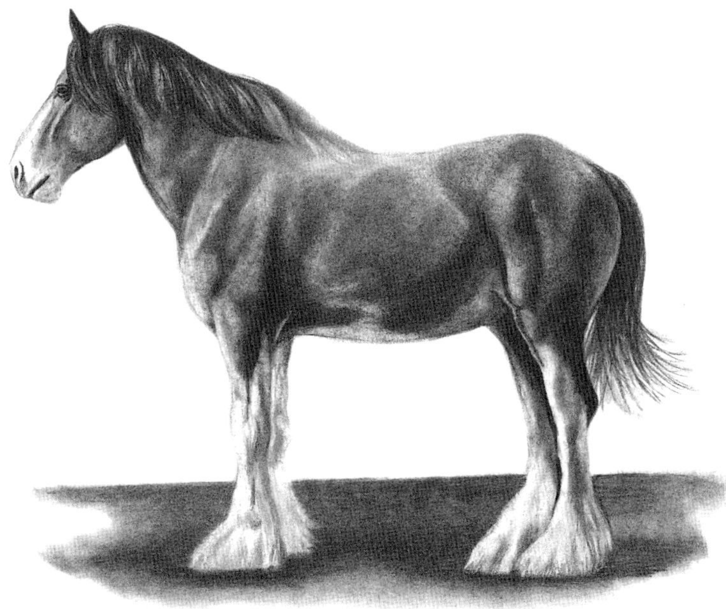

The stocky body and huge hairy feet of this horse tell us that it is a Clydesdale. Its oversized hooves have become a trademark for the breed, signifying its strength.

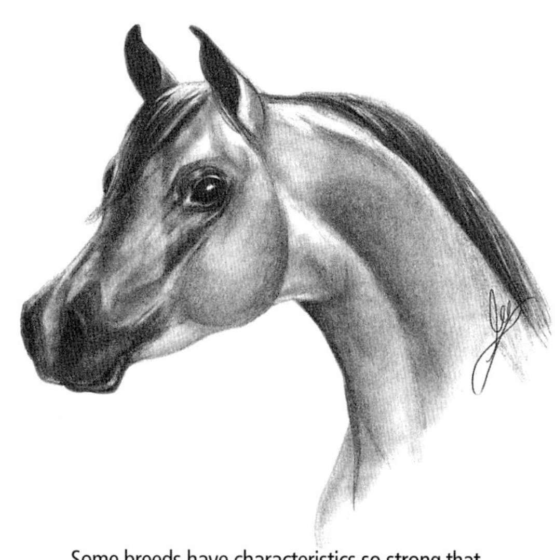

Some breeds have characteristics so strong that they are easily recognized. They have become a stereotype for their breed. For instance, the small, dished face and narrow curved neck of this horse automatically tells us it is an Arabian. No other horse has this look.

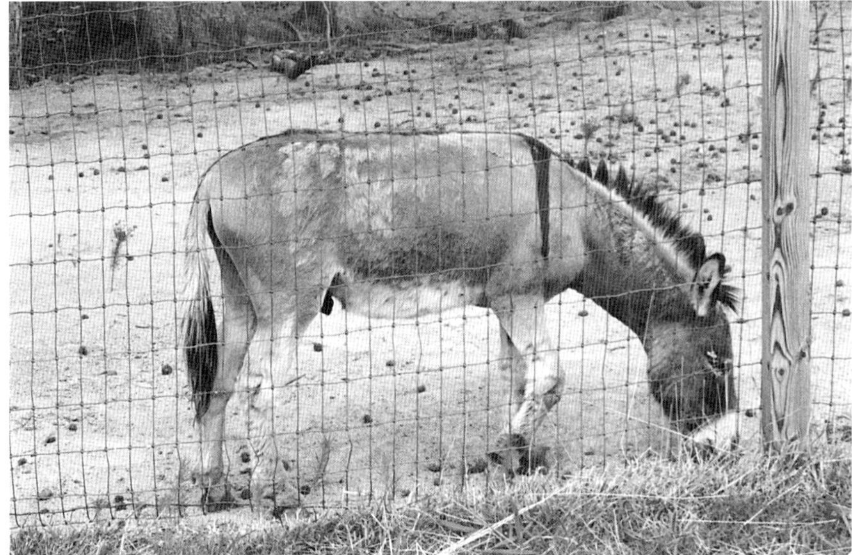

At a small zoo, I found these little guys. This is a burro. It is another very recognizable workhorse. Its gray color and dark face and tail are traditional for this breed. Notice how different the tail appears when compared to the tail of a horse.

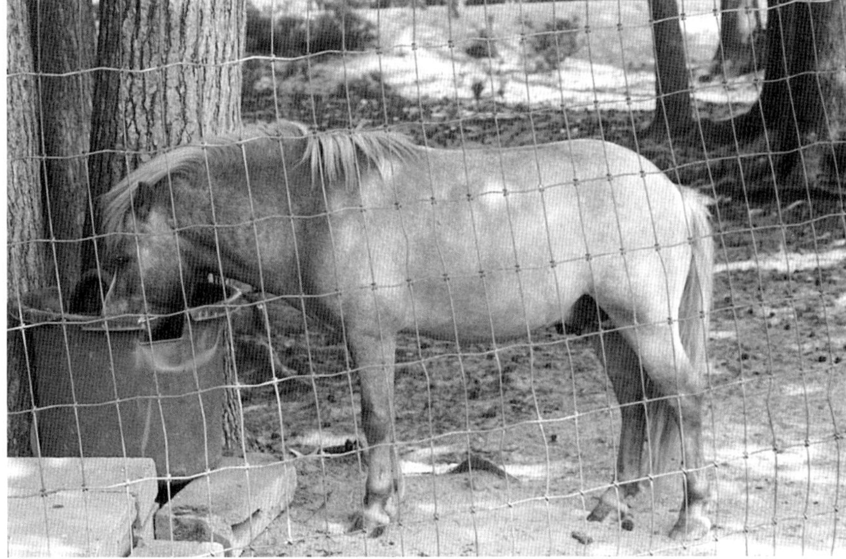

This pony is a cutie, with its short legs and stocky body. Look at how different the body shape is when compared to the burro. The pony is much rounder and fuller.

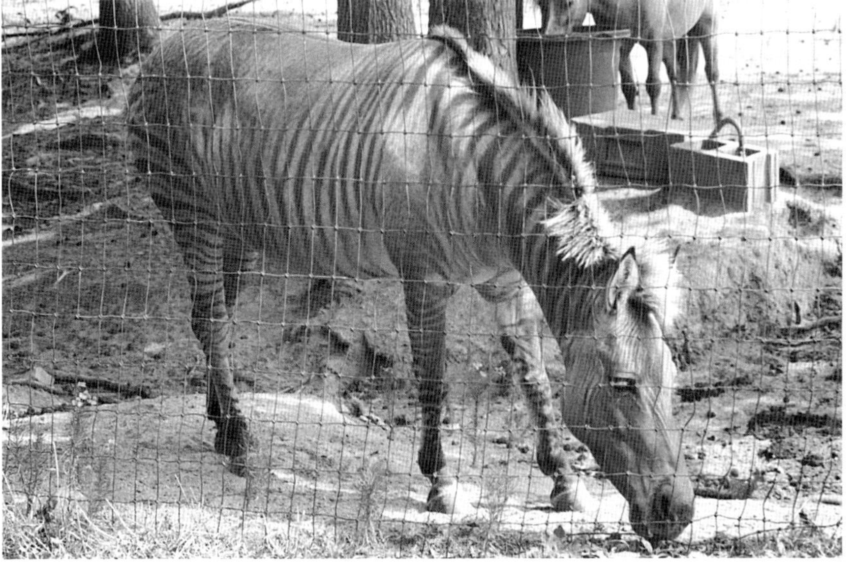

I couldn't believe my eyes when I saw this animal. I thought for sure that the sun was getting to me! But it is just what it looks like. It is a zee-donk! It is half zebra and half donkey. I didn't think it was possible either, but here is the proof. You can see characteristics of both breeds in it. The colors were fascinating, with the shades of brown and the subtle zebra stripes. He makes for a very interesting subject, don't you think?

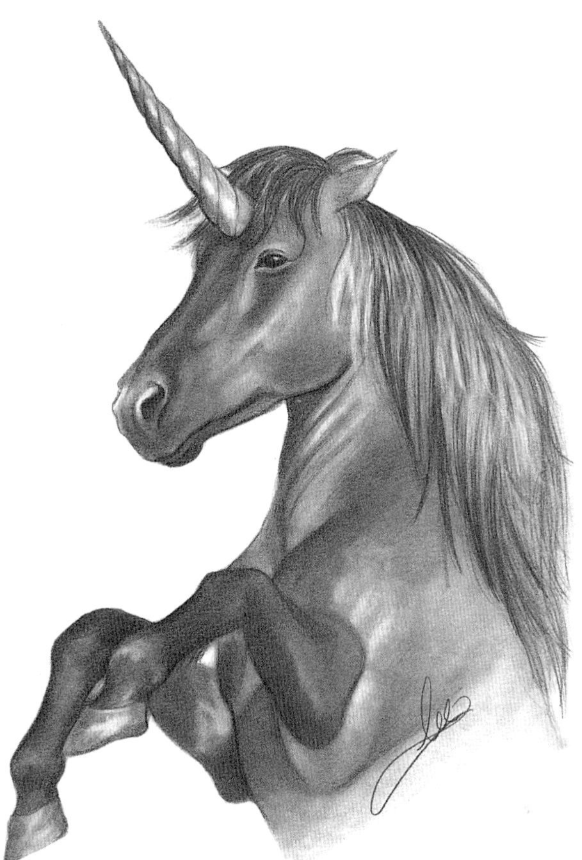

Sometimes it is fun to create images from your own imagination, or combine elements from different photographs. That is what I did for this drawing. Later in the book you will see a drawing I did of a horse rearing. When looking at that pose, I imagined it a different way. I drew it again and changed it. The first creation was simple enough. I merely added a twisted horn and turned the horse into a Unicorn.

I then got a little more creative, and drew it a third time. I wanted this one to look like Pegasus. This time, I wanted to be more precise in my drawing so I looked at some pictures I had of birds. I borrowed the wings from one of them and combined it with the horse. I wanted the picture to have further eye appeal, so I placed the moon behind the horse to enhance it.

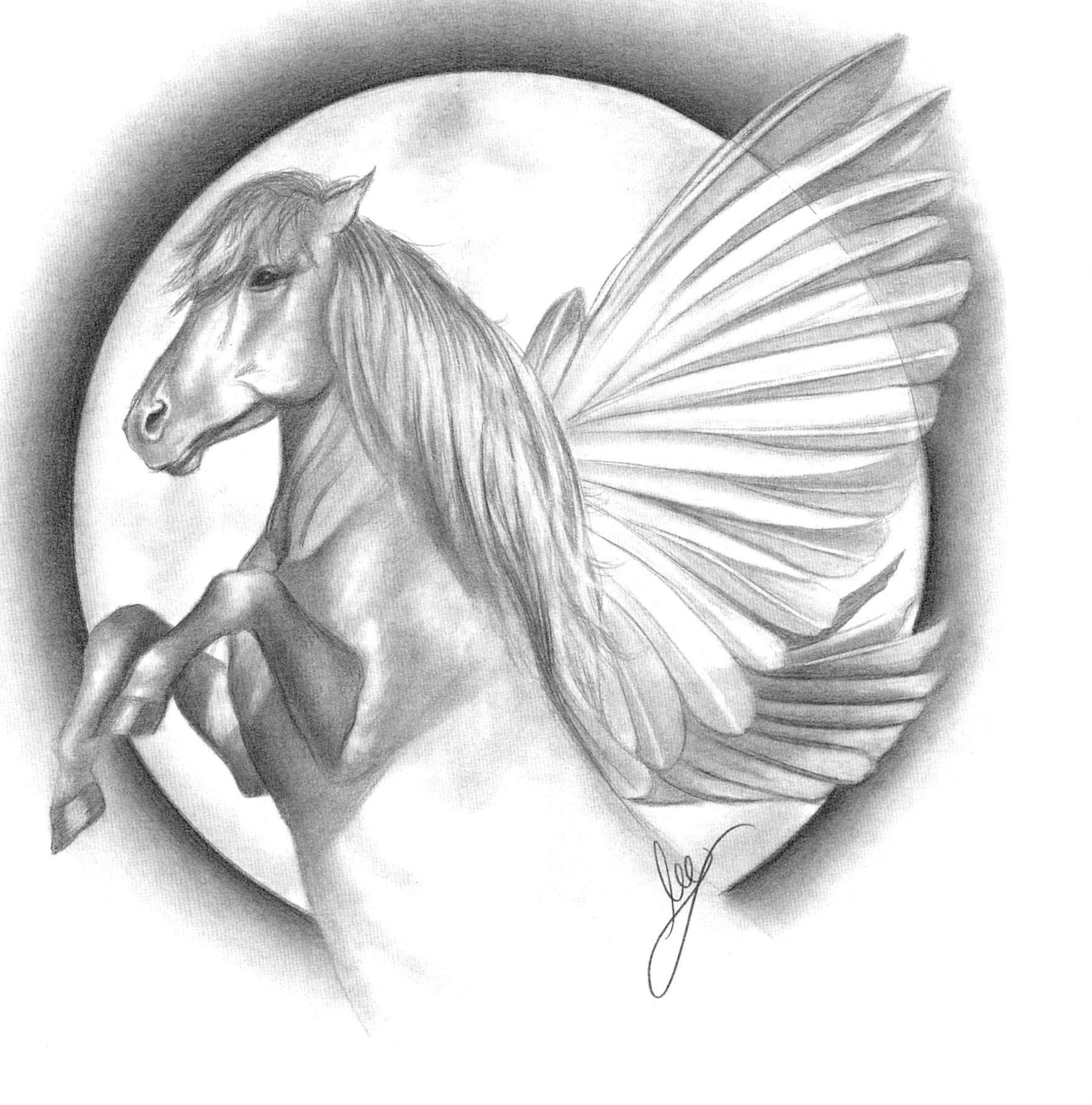

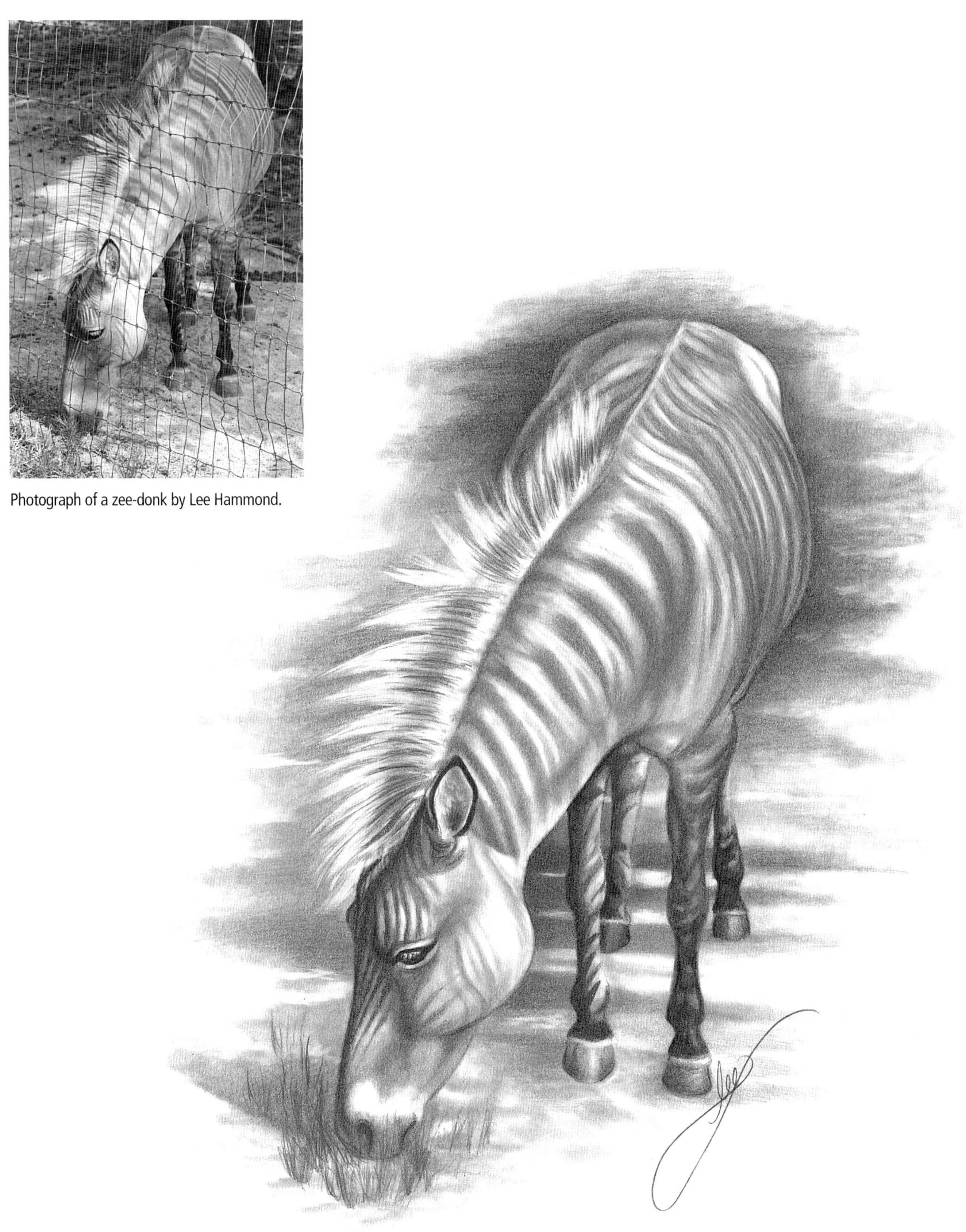

Photograph of a zee-donk by Lee Hammond.

This is an example of the type of drawing you can do from your own photographs. This is a complex piece due to the patterns and lighting. If you are a beginner, you might want to start with something less complicated.

Chapter Seven

Drawing Facial Features

Animals have the same life essence as people. Each creature has its own personality, and it is through the eyes that they express their feelings. Horses have beautiful eyes. I love drawing their deep color and soulful expressions.

For me, the eyes are the most critical element to any portrait. It doesn't matter if the portrait is of a person or an animal. The eyes hold all of the personality and soul of the subject. I want my drawing to communicate with viewers, making them feel like they are beholding a living thing. I use eyes as a way of connecting with my audience.

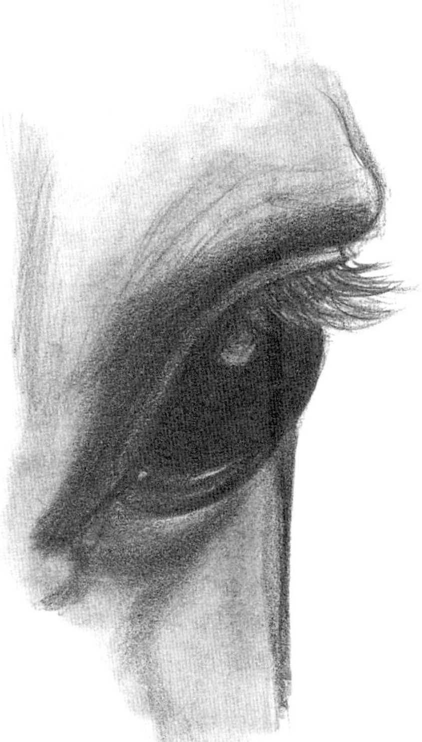

This front view shows the beautiful eyelashes horses have. This characteristic gives the horse a human quality that we can identify with. The lashes are only visible from this view. The side view below makes them hard to see.

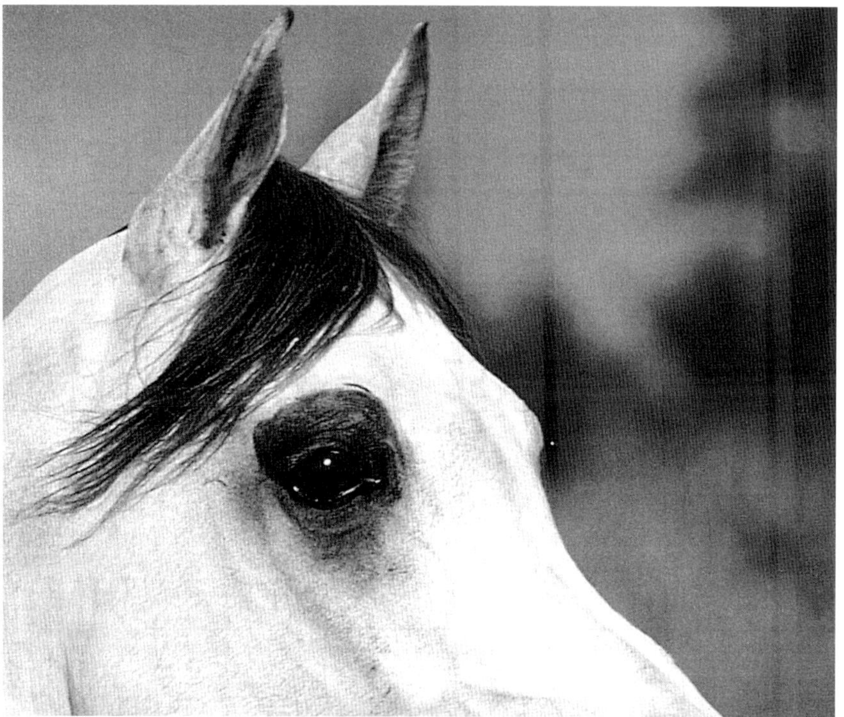

This close-up of a horse's eye shows all of the details necessary to make your drawing of a horse come to life. Study it well, and look at all of the small areas of creases, highlights and shadows. Follow the exercise on the next page to draw this eye realistically.

THE SINGLE EYE

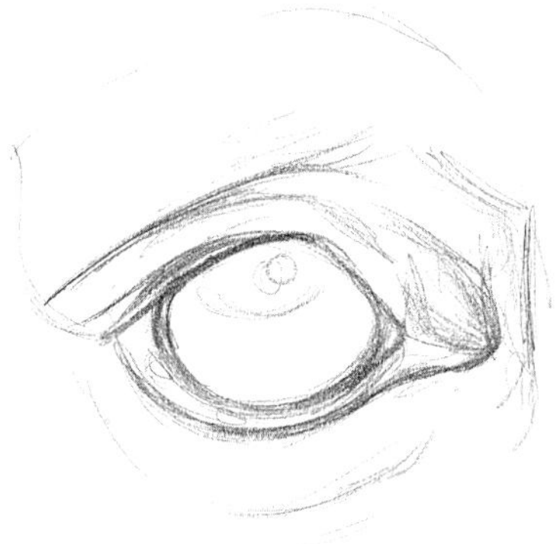

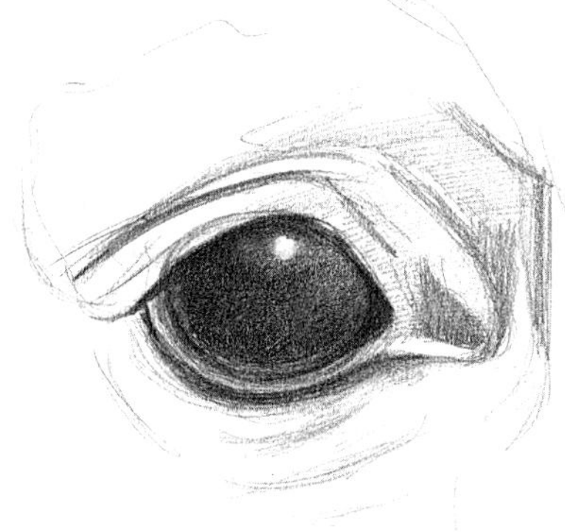

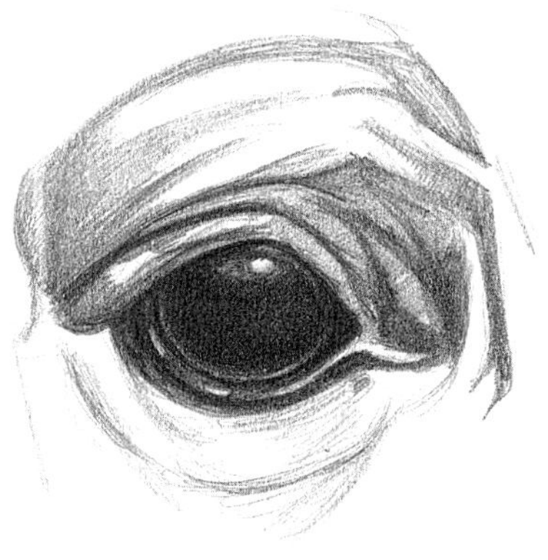

STEP 1
Create a line drawing like this. You can use a graph overlay, or freehand your shapes.

STEP 2
Darken inside the eye. Do not cover up the highlighted area. (This is also called a "catch-light.") The eye is darker in the center where the pupil is. Resist the urge to fill in the whole eye. This will make it look flat. The pupil is just not as noticeable or defined as in a human eye. You need some variation in the tones here. Start to place some tone in the shapes around the eye. These areas are not as dark as the eyeball area.

STEP 3
Continue adding tone around the eye, paying attention to the creases and shadows.

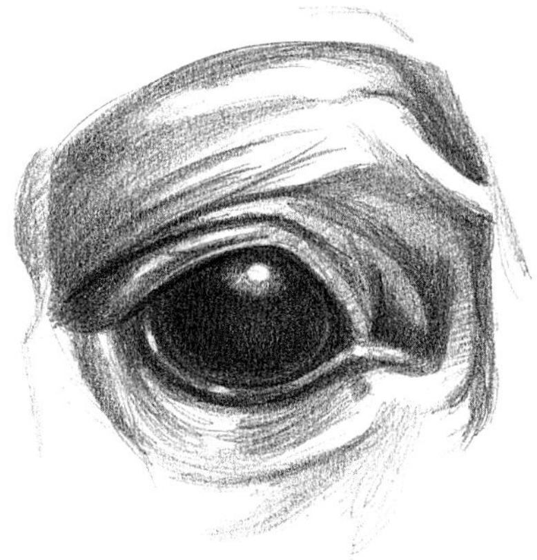

STEP 4
With your tortillion, begin blending the tones to soften them. Blend the eyeball, and add more graphite to deepen the tones. Lift the catchlight out with the kneaded eraser. This is what will make the eye look shiny.

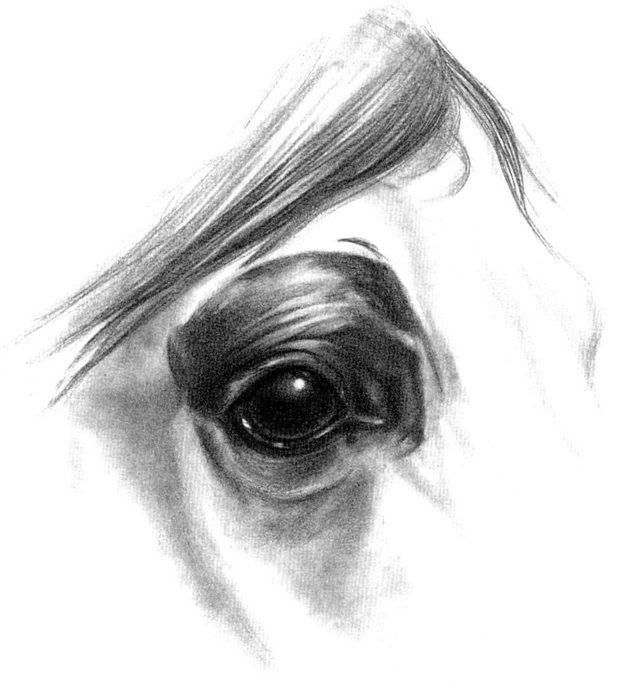

STEP 5
By adding some of the details of the face surrounding the eye, the drawing looks much more realistic. Blend the facial tones with a dirty tortillion for softness. I will show you how to draw the forelock in a later chapter.

PAIRS OF EYES

It is very important to not only know how to draw eyes, but to know how to draw two eyes together. Both eyes must appear to be looking in the same direction, and be of the same size and shape. The turn of the head, or a change of direction will alter the way the eyes appear.

The eyes of a horse are very far apart, resting on the outside of the head. They protrude from the face causing a noticeable bulge. Notice how the eyelids stretch over the eyeball. Study the two views on this page, and you will see how different they are from those of a person. You do not see the white of the eye (sclera) as you do with a human eye. The colored part of the eye is much larger in animals.

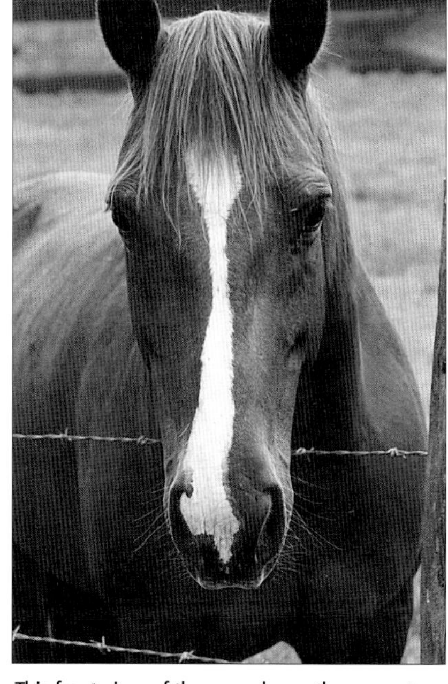

This front view of the eyes shows the accurate placement of them. They are very wide set, resting on the side of the face.

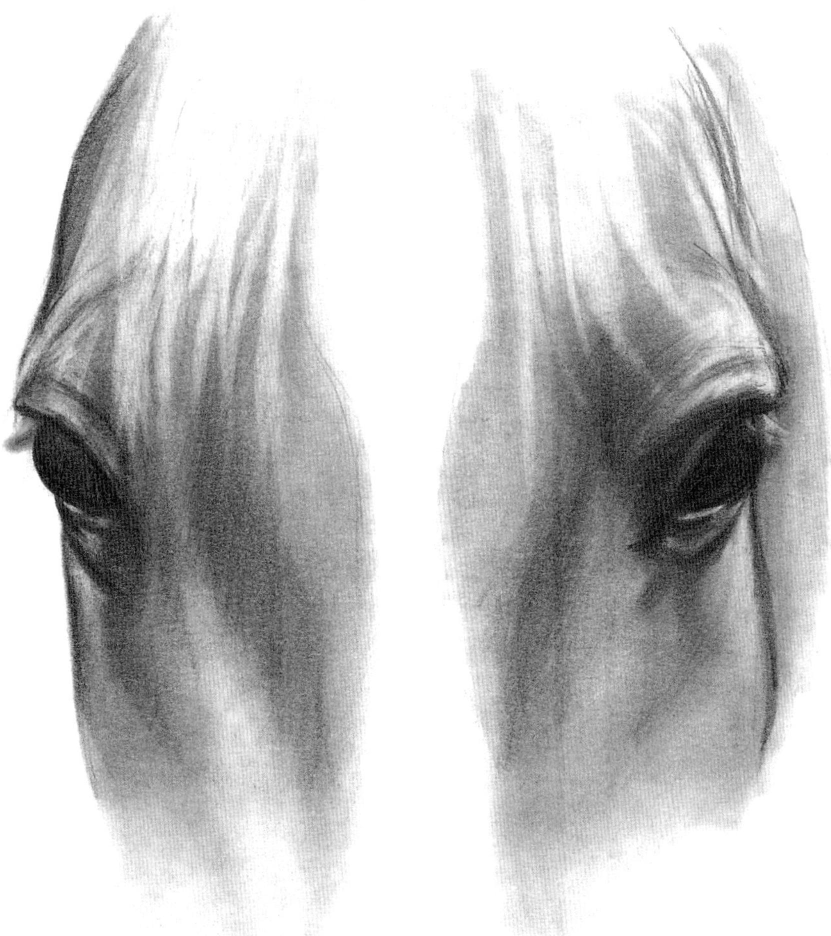

This drawing is a good example of the way eyes look when they are viewed from the front. I used patterns of light and dark to create them. Look at where the eyes bulge, and you will see where I lifted light. Areas of the face that recede appear darker. If you follow the instructions on the next page, you too will be able to draw eyes as realistic as these.

EYE EXERCISES

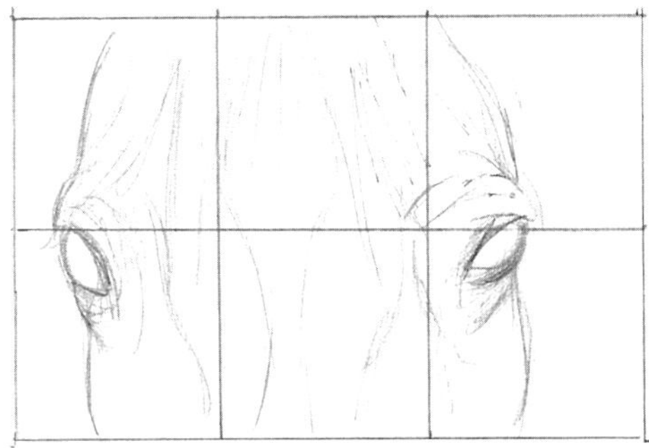

STEP 1

Lightly draw a grid on your drawing paper. For this you will need six one-inch squares. Draw the shapes you see in each box until your drawing looks like mine.

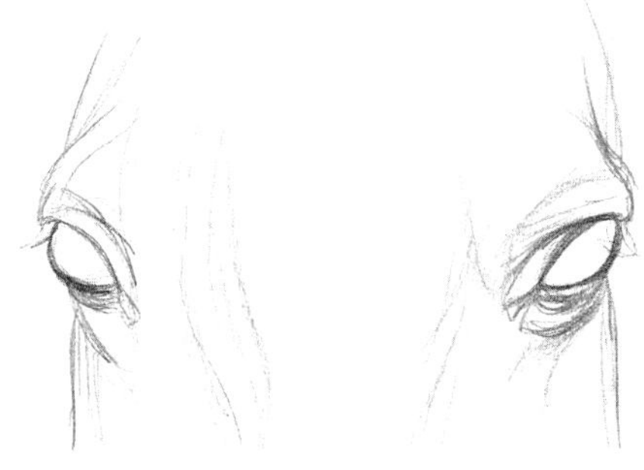

STEP 2

When you are sure of the accuracy of your drawing, gently remove your grid lines with the kneaded eraser, and proceed to the next step.

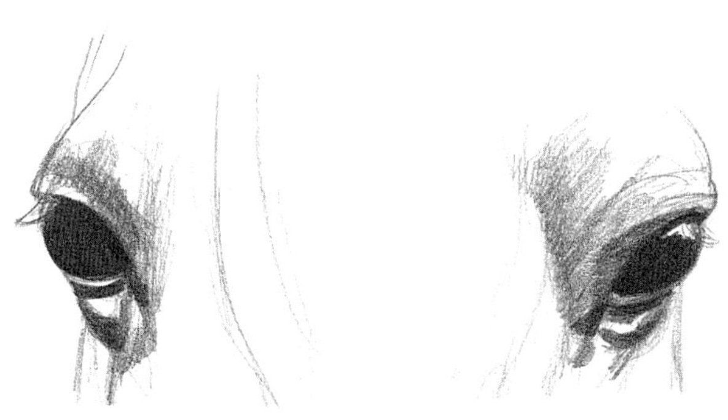

STEP 3

Apply the darkest tones to the eyeballs. Because of the light direction, and the shadows of the eyelids, there is no catchlight visible. Leave the small area light where the eyelashes appear. Begin to place some tone around the eye.

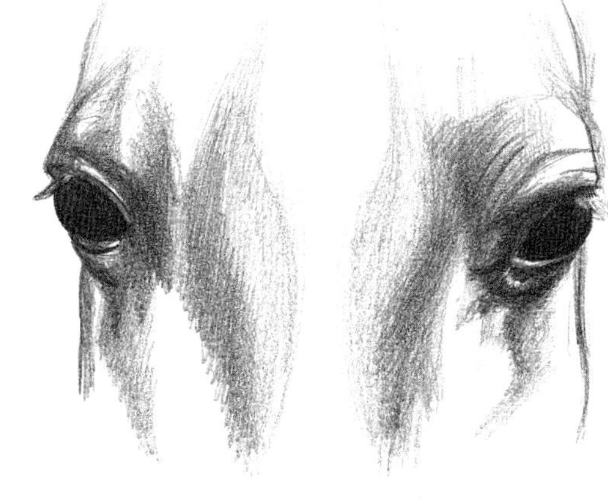

STEP 4

Develop the tones of the face. This is what creates the bone structure. Look at these areas as patterns of light and dark.

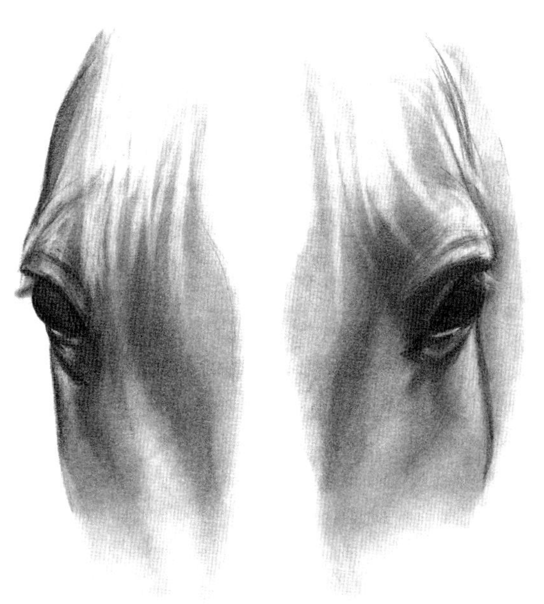

STEP 5

Blend your drawing with the tortillion to smooth and soften the look. Lift all of the light areas back out with a piece of your kneaded eraser rolled into a point. This always makes the light areas seem more reflective and natural. Also lift the forelock with the kneaded eraser. To create long streaks such as this, flatten a piece of your eraser between your thumb and forefinger. With quick, long strokes, lift the areas of light to look like hair. Repeat the flattening procedure after every two or three strokes to clean and refresh your eraser. The quicker the stroke, the more the end will taper. This makes it look more like hair strands.

NOSES AND MOUTHS

When I teach the facial features for drawing portraits of people, I have students practice each feature separately. This gives them the experience they need before putting all of the features together. This is hard to do with horses. Although the eyes are separate, the nose and mouth are closely related. It is impossible to draw one without the other.

It is important to examine and study how different the features look when viewed from different angles. The shapes of the nostrils look entirely different from the front than they do from the side.

When looking at the nostrils from the front, the shape appears as a teardrop. But like any living thing, this will vary from individual to individual, and breed to breed. Study your photo carefully for these shapes, before you begin your drawing.

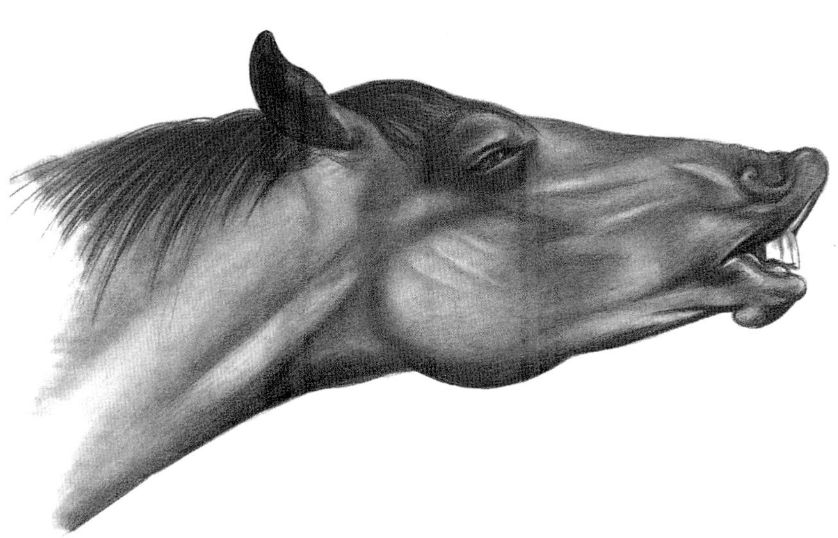

The nose and mouth of a horse are connected, so it is impossible to draw one without the other.

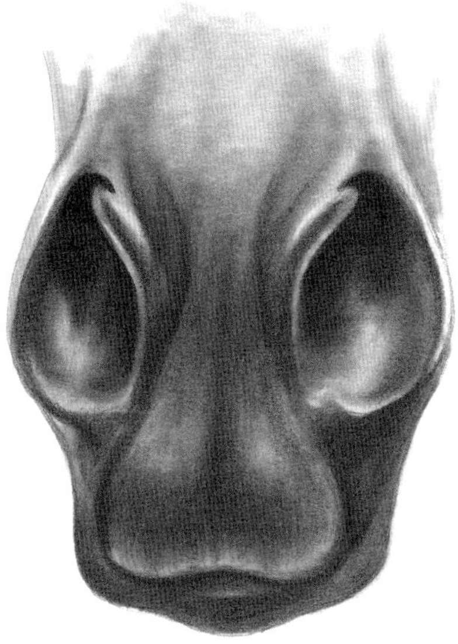

From the front view, the nostrils appear symmetrical. They will be the same shape. The shape of the nostril connects to the mouth.

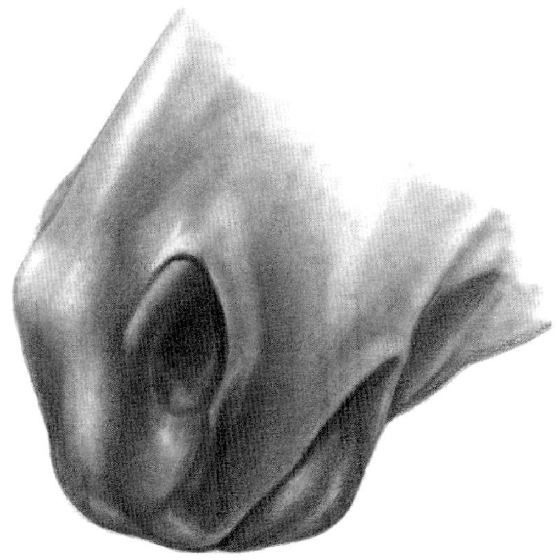

The nostril is a shape that has many other shapes within it. Each horse's nostril area will be different.

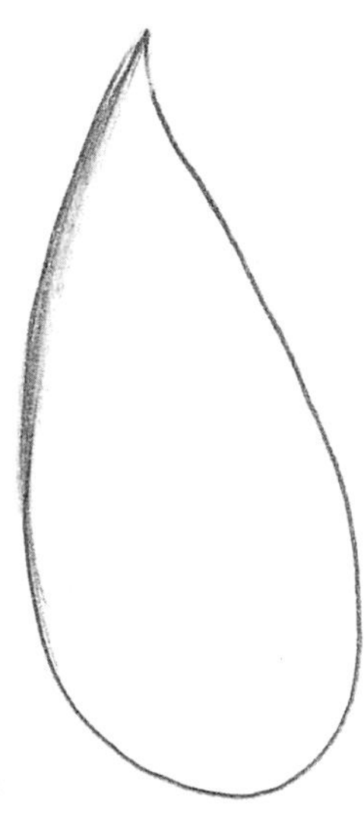

The shape of the nostril closely resembles a teardrop.

NOSE EXERCISES

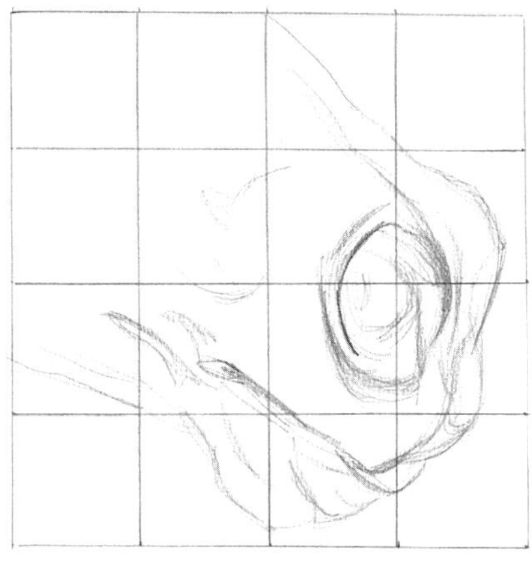

STEP 1
Use eight one-inch boxes for your grid. When your line drawing looks like mine, remove your graph lines.

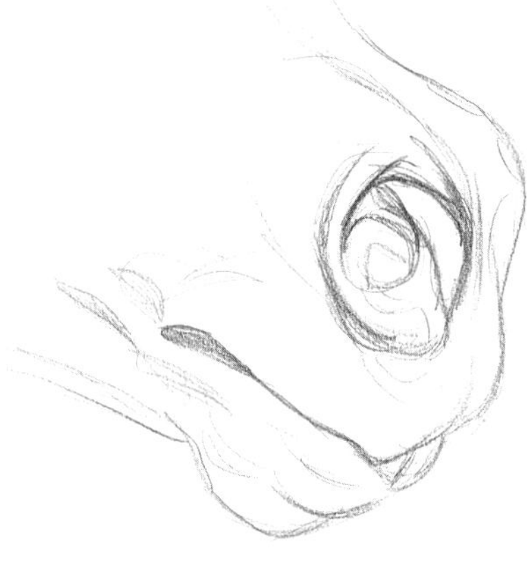

STEP 2
An accurate line drawing with the graph removed.

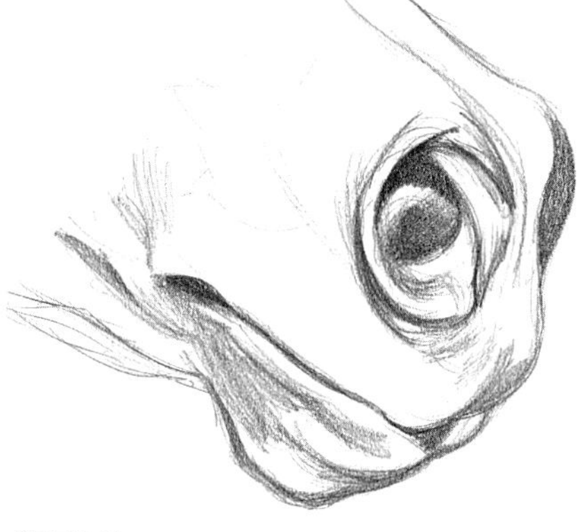

STEP 3
Begin placing in the darkest areas first. Look at the tones as patterns of light and dark, assigning each shape its own tone. At this stage it resembles a puzzle.

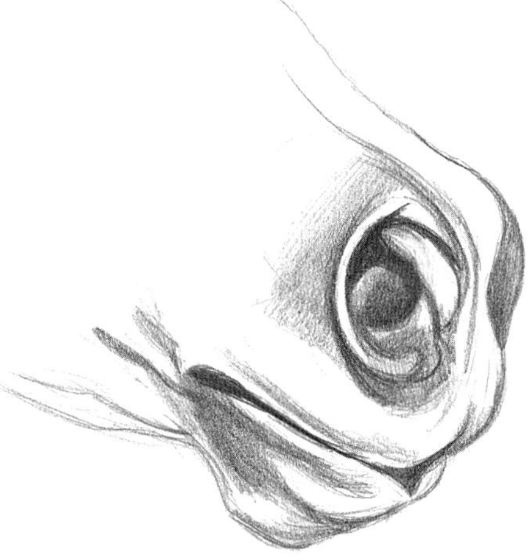

STEP 4
Continue adding the tones. These create the halftone areas.

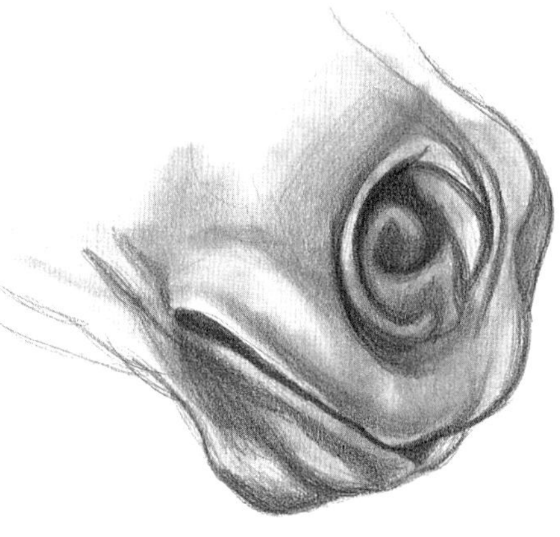

STEP 5
Blend the tones out with your tortillion. This will smooth out the tones, making them appear softer.

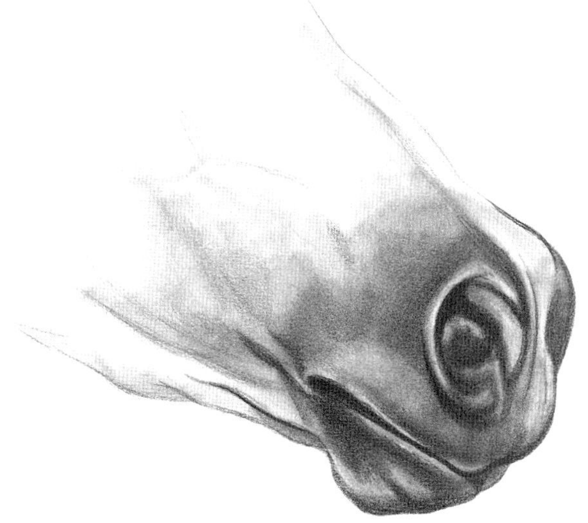

STEP 6
Gently lift out some of the lighter areas with the kneaded eraser. This should be done to the rim of the nostril, the edge of the upper lip and the chin area. If any of the tones were lightened during the blending phase, deepen them once again, and blend.

EARS

Each breed has similarities and extreme differences. The ears are areas that differ quite a bit. Look at these examples and you will see the different shapes, sizes and colors. Look at each one carefully to see the characteristics unique to each horse breed.

Look through pictures and drawings of as many different types and poses of ears as possible. It is always better practice to draw the features individually than to work on the entire horse right away.

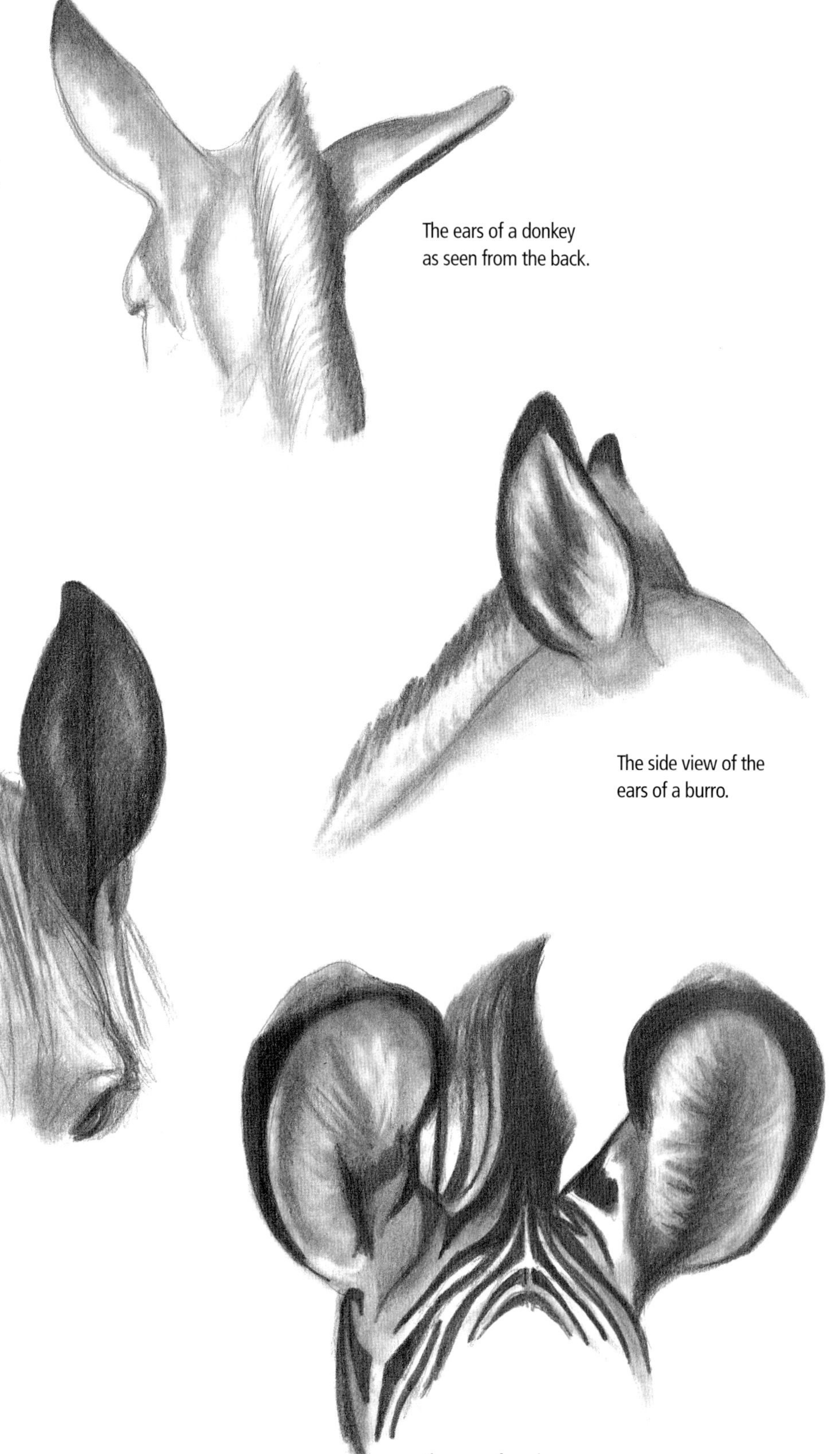

The ears of a donkey as seen from the back.

The side view of the ears of a burro.

The ears of a horse.

The ears of a zebra.

EAR EXERCISES

To practice, let's just draw one ear to learn the basic steps. Start with a light line drawing of the shapes. You can use a graph to obtain the shape, or freehand it.

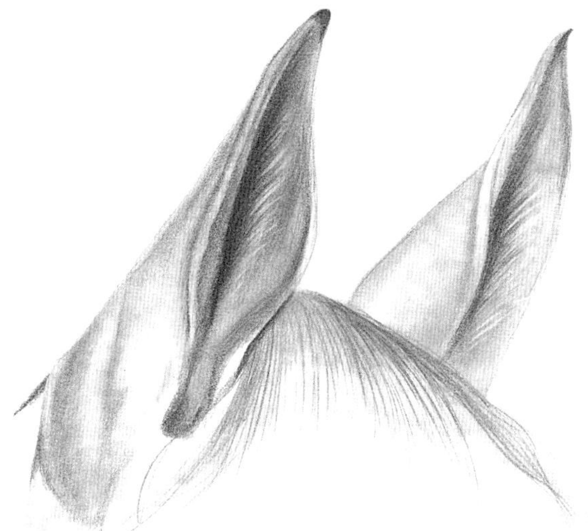

Here is a typical pose of a horse. Study the shapes of the ears. (Do you think Mr. Spock may have been related to a horse?)

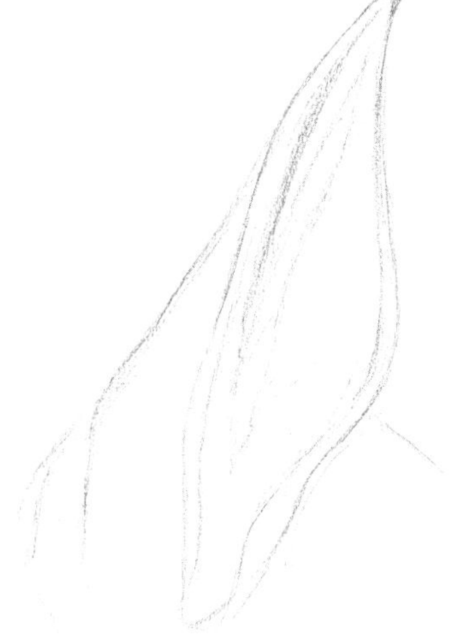

STEP 1

Use this line drawing of a single ear for practice. Freehand this shape, or place one of your acetate grids over it for accuracy.

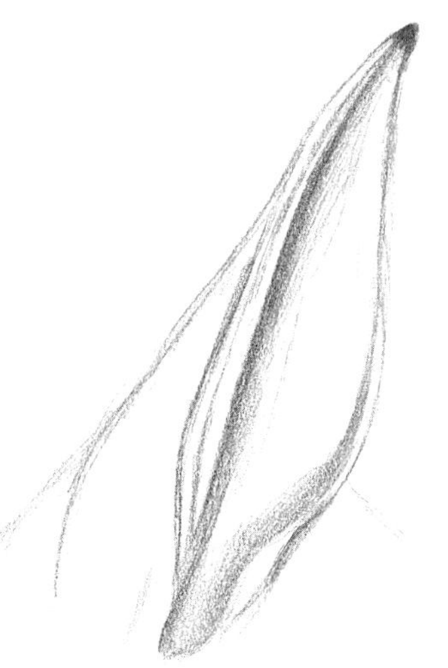

STEP 2

Starting with the inside edge of the ear, place your darkest tones. This area represents where the ear recesses into the head.

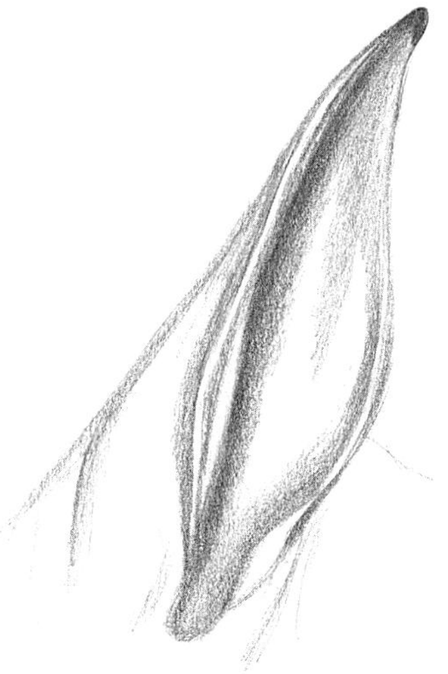

STEP 3

Continue building the tones, adding the darker tones. Refer to the photograph and my finished drawing for accurate placement.

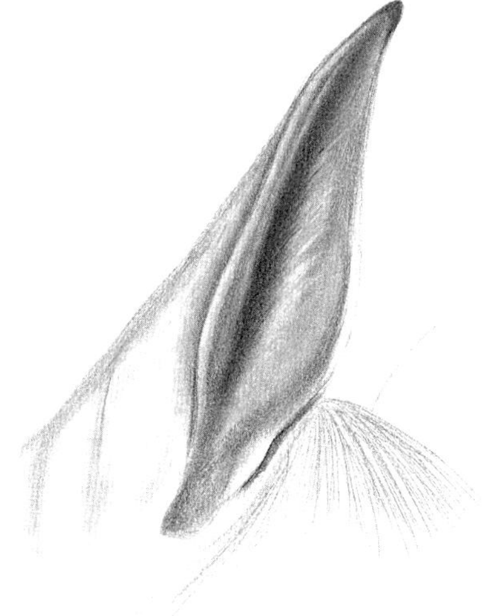

STEP 4

Blend your work out with a tortillion. This softens and smoothes the tones. The illusion of hair inside the ears was created with the kneaded eraser. Flattening the eraser into an edge and lifting the light streaks with quick strokes makes it look real. The lifted area looks like light hair against a dark area.

Chapter Eight

Drawing Horse Hair

When drawing horses, their coats appear smooth and sleek. Little of the texture of the hair is visible, and the drawing is mostly made up of light and dark patterns. But their forelocks, manes and tails are very important to the overall look of the horse, and they must be drawn with the proper amount of detail to make them look realistic.

When I draw, it always amazes me how similar things are from subject to subject. Since I view everything the same artistically—as nothing more than shapes, lights and darks— I use the same procedure when I draw. When drawing the forehead of this horse, with its forelock, I was amused that it was exactly like drawing a picture of me. We have the same hairstyle!

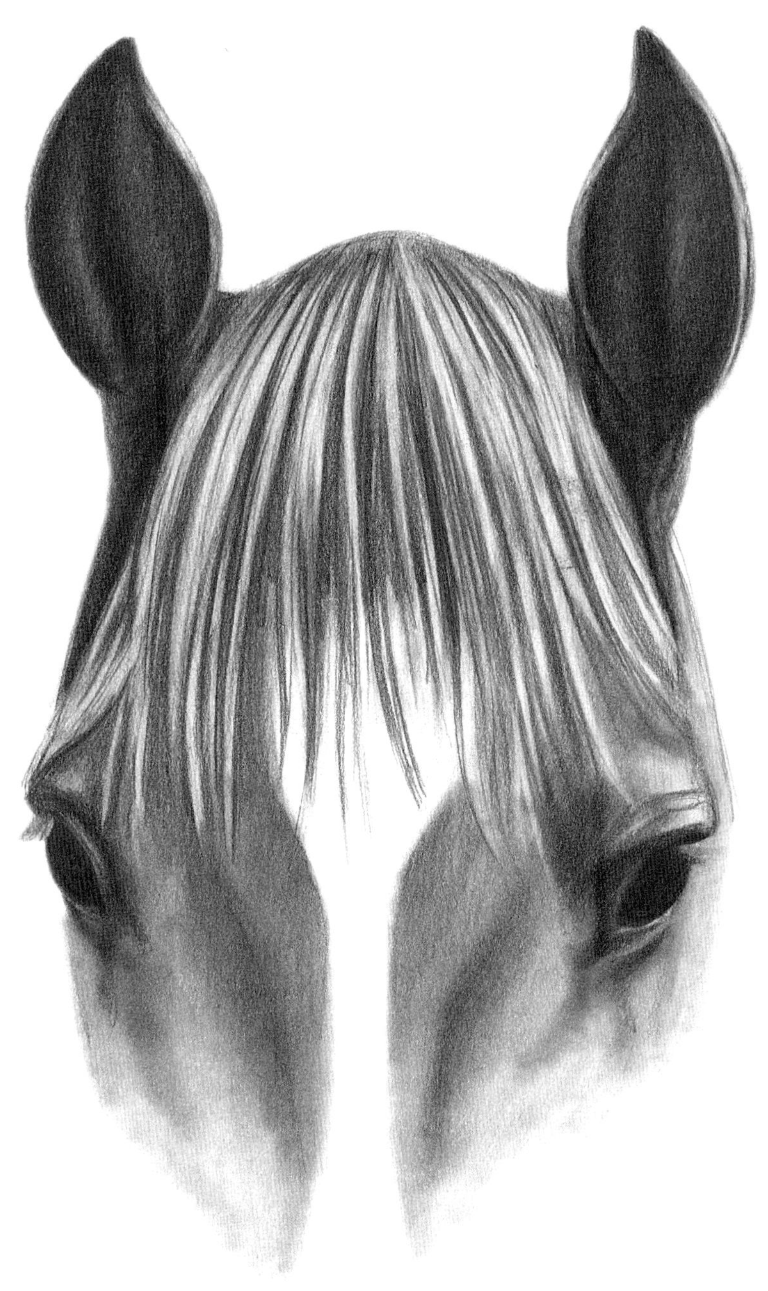

When drawing hair you must use many layers of pencil lines. The light hairs that overlap the darker ones are "lifted" with a kneaded eraser. This is done by squishing the eraser into a razor edge and stroking it across the dark tones.

THE DIFFERENT PENCIL STROKES

The most important thing about drawing hair is the type of stroke you use with your pencil. It is imperative to use a very quick flick of the wrist, and not a hard deliberate line. This takes practice!

If you try to control your lines too much, the line width appears too harsh and even and makes them look rigid and overdrawn. Quick strokes, however, make the lines taper at the end, and give a more relaxed appearance.

Because hair grows in layers of thousands of hair strands, you must apply many pencil strokes to create that look. Draw lines quickly that overlap one another, until you fill in the hair area.

Then by blending the drawing with the tortillion, you'll remove the white of the paper from between the pencil lines. This is important, since hair casts a shadow under itself. You would not see white skin between your hair strands, so you do not need the white showing in your drawing.

Finally, lighten the drawing by using the kneaded eraser. Flatten the eraser between your thumb and forefinger to create a razor edge. Using that same quick stroke, lift some light hairs from the drawing.

Take a look at these examples of both long and short hair, and see how this simple three-step process achieves stunning results.

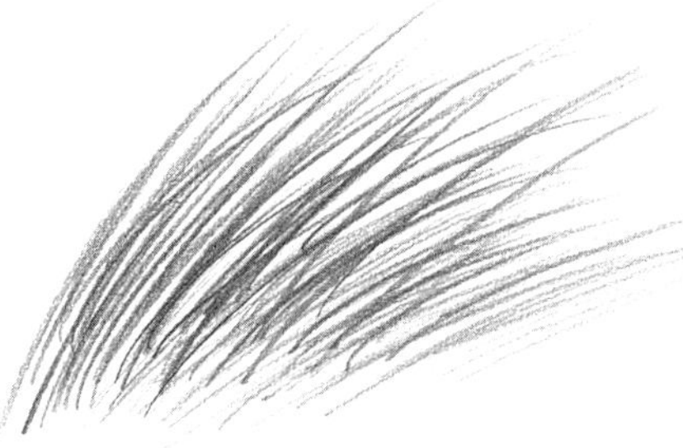

Long Hair: Apply Quick Strokes
It is important to layer your quick pencil lines to help fill the hair in. These lines overlap one another creating the illusion of hair.

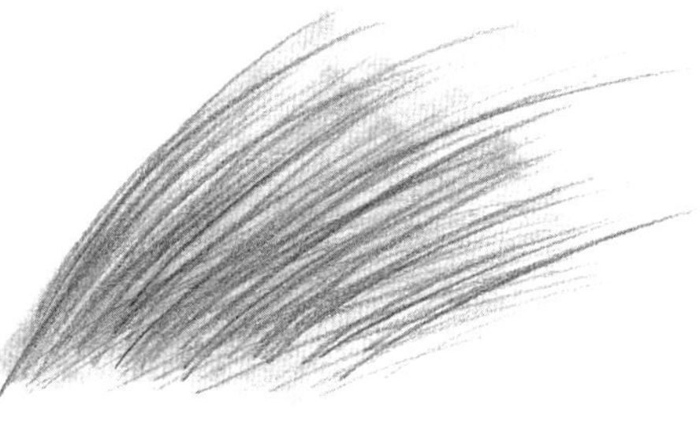

Long Hair: Blend
Blending out the white of the paper will help the hair look more realistic. You do not want white paper to show between your pencil lines.

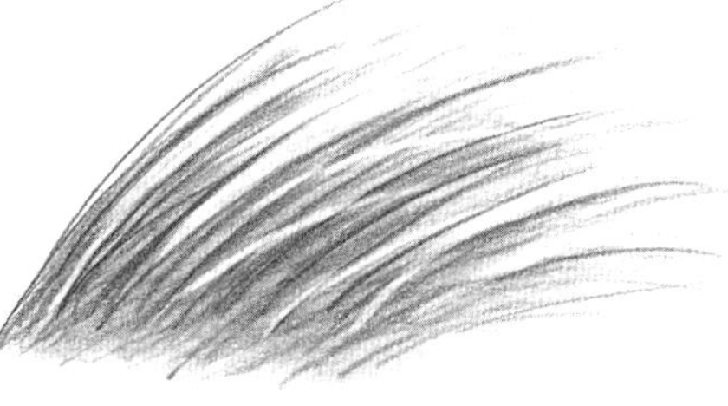

Long Hair: Lift
Lifting out the light highlights and light hairs with the kneaded eraser will make the hair look layered and realistic.

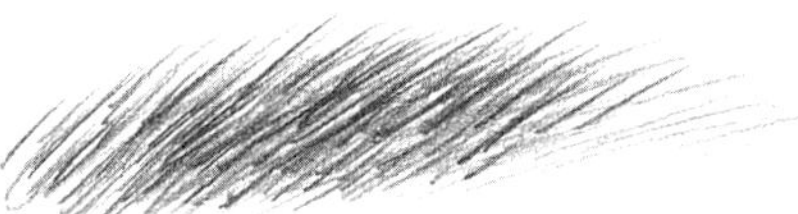

Short Hair: Apply Quick Strokes
Applying very short, quick strokes will produce the look of short hair. The quicker you apply the pencil marks, the more the lines taper at the ends.

Short Hair: Blend
Gently blend to remove the white of the paper.

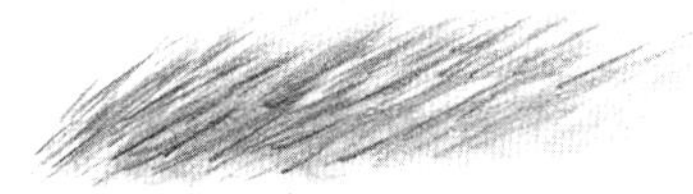

Short Hair: Lift
The kneaded eraser will lift out the light hair and highlights.

Basing the tone in with a dirty tortillion can create the look of soft hair. The lighter hairs are then lifted off the top with a kneaded eraser.

DRAWING MANES

Manes are created much the same way as in the previous exercises. The difference is the curve of the hair. When drawing hair, all of the pencil lines must imitate the growth of the hair. If the hair is curling, or wavy, your pencil lines must be applied in the same direction.

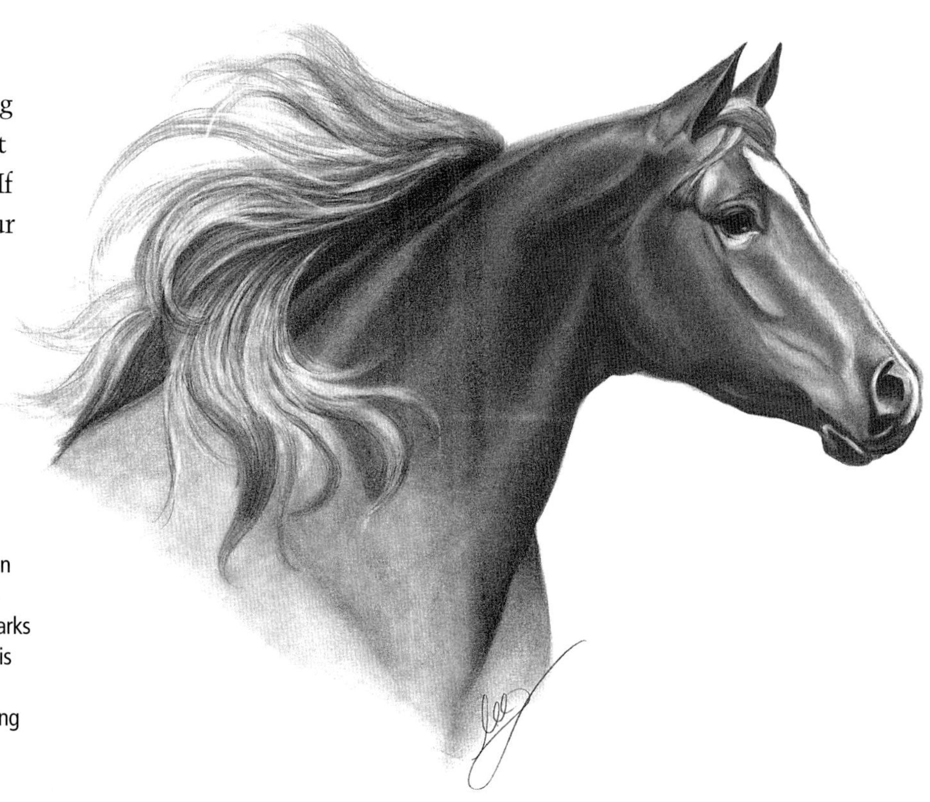

Applying the pencil lines in a curved direction creates the look of flowing hair. Wavy hair is created with wavy pencil lines. The pencil marks should always imitate the direction the hair is moving or growing. In this drawing, it is the mane that gives the horse the illusion of being in motion.

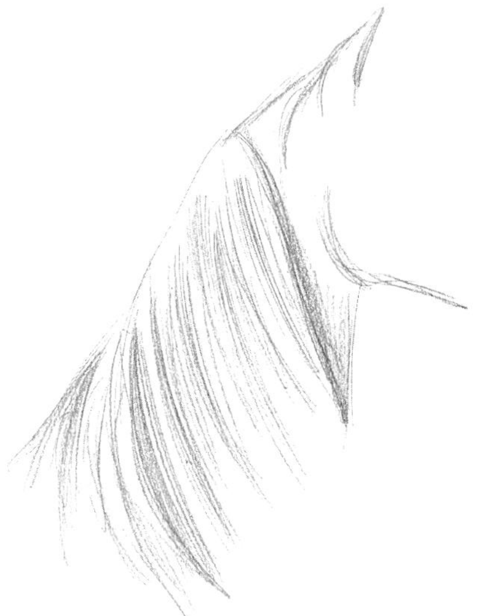

Step 1
Begin drawing the mane by lightly drawing in the overall shape. Then, begin applying the pencil strokes in the direction of the hair itself. Look for the dark areas, and fill them in first.

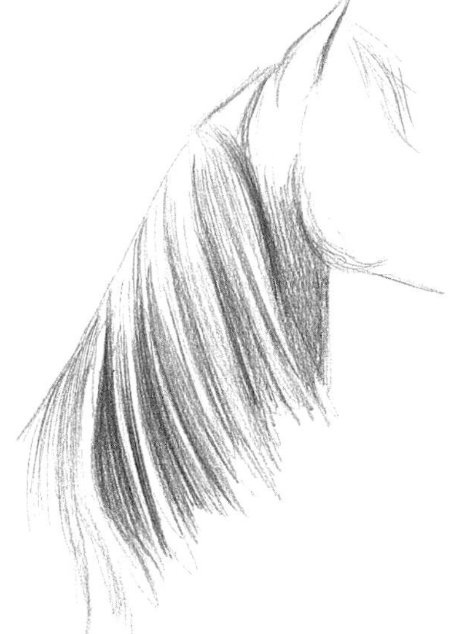

Step 2
Continue adding pencil strokes to build up the layers. Add tone to darken the neck area. This will give the lighter hair something to show up against.

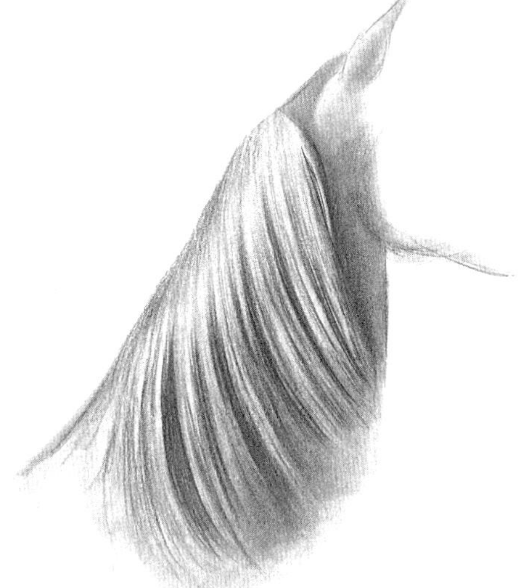

Step 3
Blend out the tones with a tortillion. Lift the light highlights of the mane with your kneaded eraser. Remember to use a flattened eraser and a quick "flick" with your stroke.

MANE EXERCISES

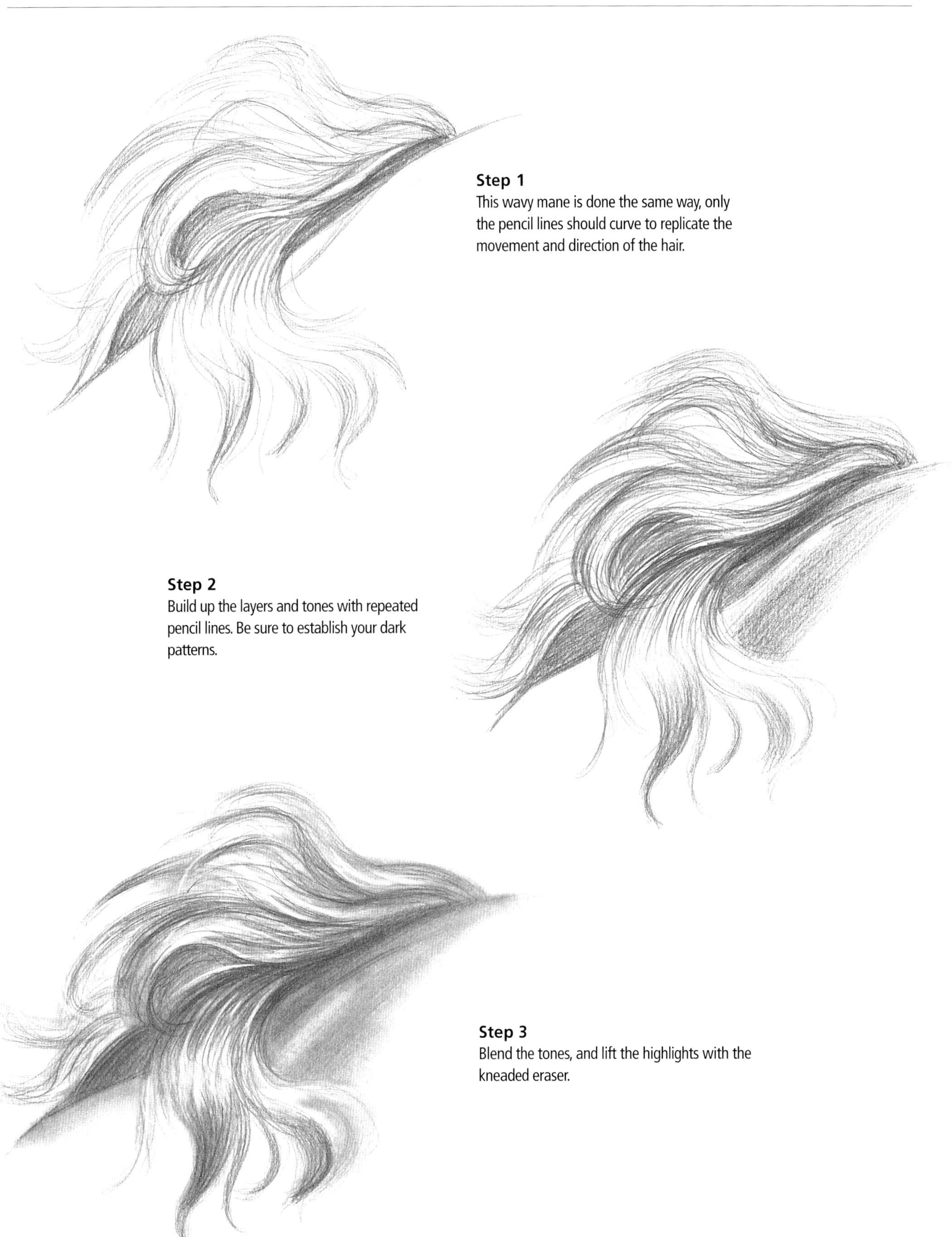

Step 1
This wavy mane is done the same way, only the pencil lines should curve to replicate the movement and direction of the hair.

Step 2
Build up the layers and tones with repeated pencil lines. Be sure to establish your dark patterns.

Step 3
Blend the tones, and lift the highlights with the kneaded eraser.

DRAWING TAILS

Drawing a horsetail is very similar to drawing a mane. There is just more hair, and it is longer. Once again, each breed has its own characteristics, so study your photo for the details.

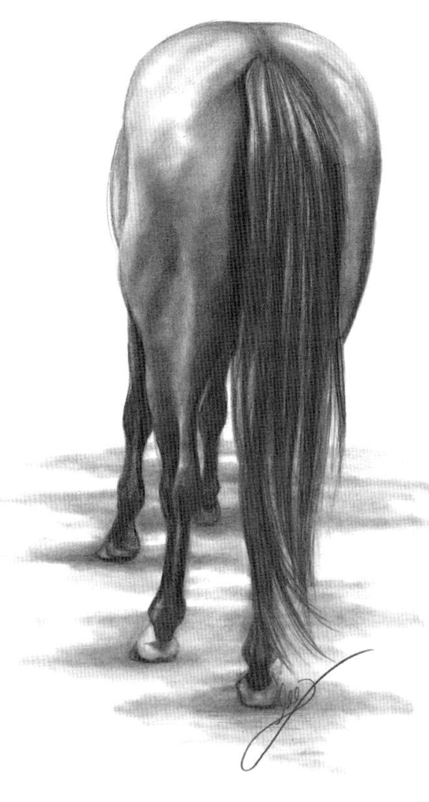

This horse has an extremely long tail. Its dark color contrasts against the body of the horse. It also casts a shadow onto the horse's back leg. Look for the areas that overlap at the end of the tail. Can you see how this gives the illusion of layers and movement, as if the tail is swishing? Also, look at how I used the kneaded eraser to lift out the light hair strands and reflections. It looks very realistic.

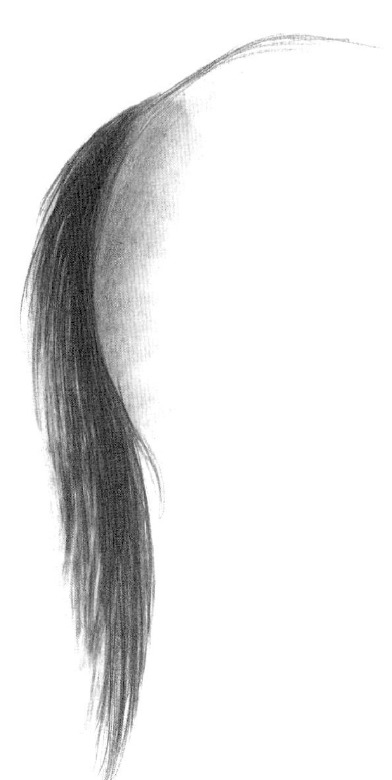

This is what a horsetail looks like from the side. The gentle curve of the rump is seen in the curve of the tail.

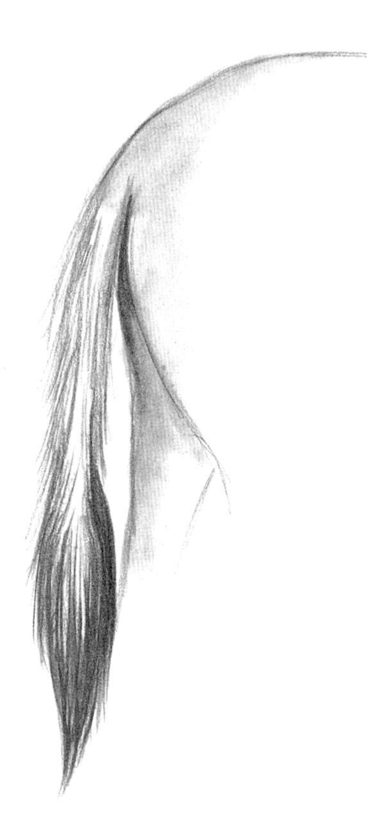

The tail of a burro resembles a zebra in its shape. The tail is smooth except for the tip.

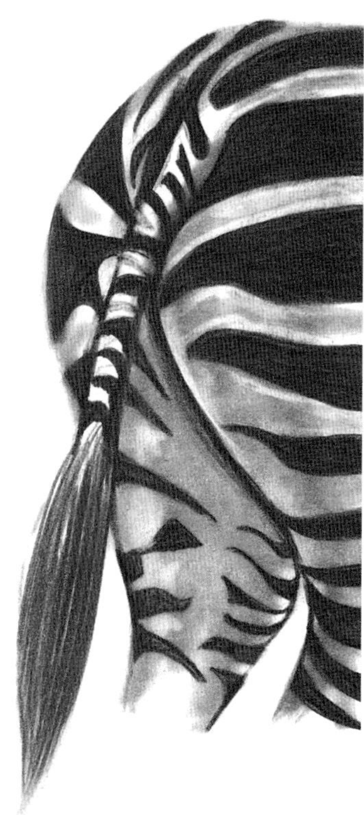

The tail of a zebra looks quite different than that of a horse. It is smooth starting at the base and is only hairy at the tip. The stripes of the zebra carry over onto the tail.

TAIL EXERCISES

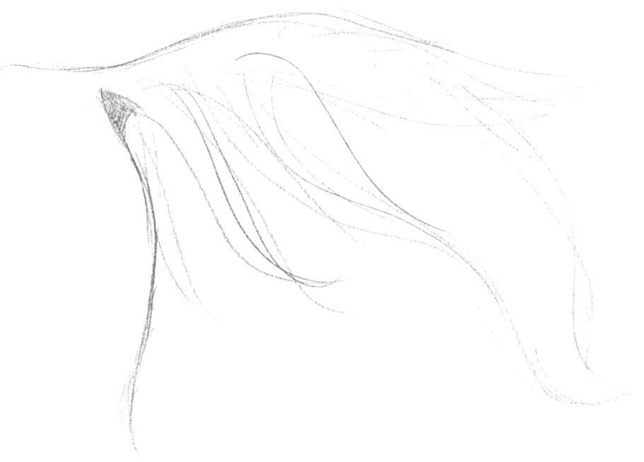

Step 1
Begin with a basic outline that depicts the shape of the tail. These lines should reflect the direction the hair is going. The waviness and movement of this tail are created solely by the direction of the pencil lines.

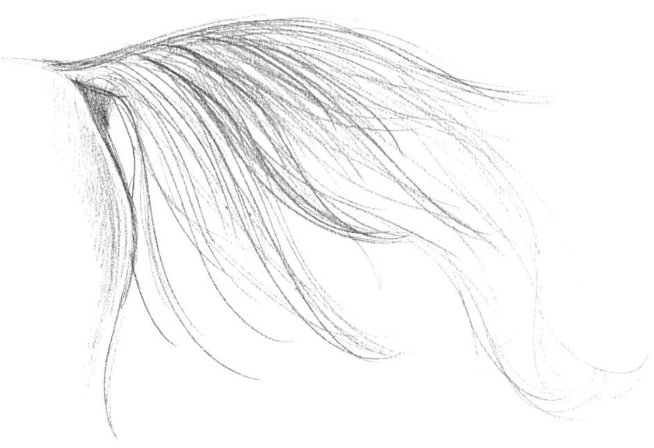

Step 2
Continue filling in the tail with wavy pencil lines.

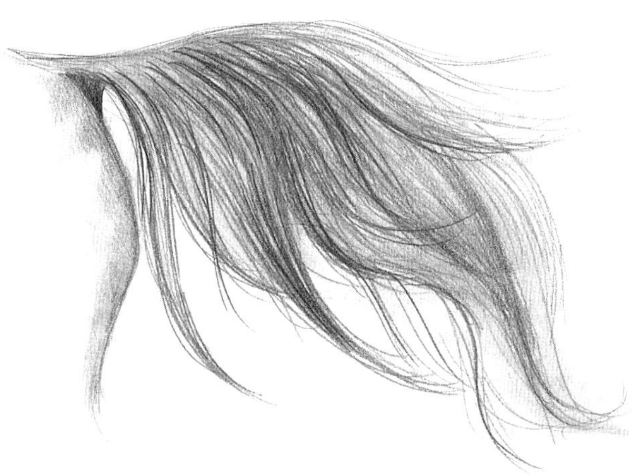

Step 3
Blend the tail with the tortillion to remove the white of the paper.

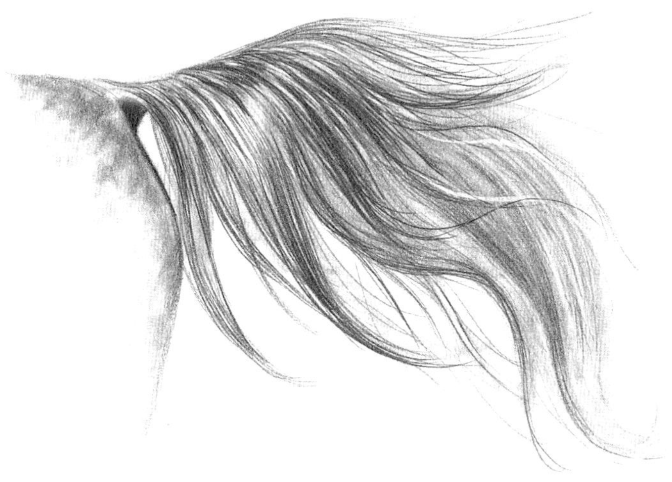

Step 4
Lift lighter colored hairs with the kneaded eraser using the same wavy direction. These light lines should overlap the others to create a layered appearance.

Chapter Nine

Drawing the Face

We have now covered all the individual facial features of a horse and how to draw them with a realistic approach. It is not necessary to draw the entire horse to make a good drawing. Beautiful compositions can be created just using the head and shoulders. In reality, I prefer this type of composition as opposed to the other, just because it captures more of the horse's personality. I try to tell the viewer about the horse's feelings and demeanor, more than just what it looks like. A portrait of the face allows me to do this.

PROJECT 1

Let's begin with this photograph of a head. Refer to the previous chapters, and review the procedure for drawing the eyes, nose and mouth. Follow the step-by-step instructions to create this portrait.

Although this is a fairly simple drawing, it has a lot of appeal due to the gentleness of the horse's personality. When taking pictures for the book, I just happened to come across this horse and another in a pasture. They came right up to the fence, wanting me to pet them. This one was the friendliest. He nudged my ear and almost ate my camera strap!

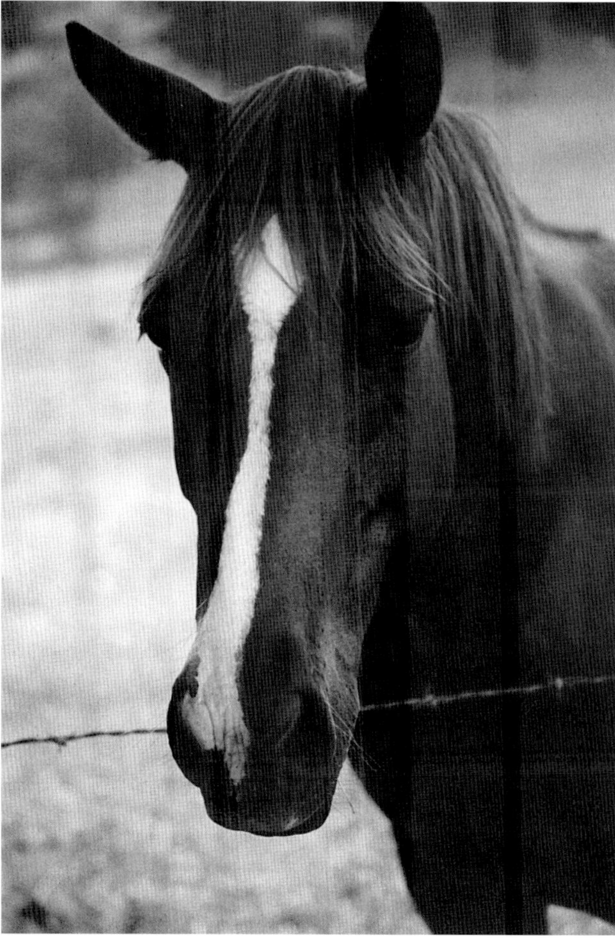

This photo will give you practice drawing a dark colored horse. This type of pose has a lot of expression, and shows the horse's personality.

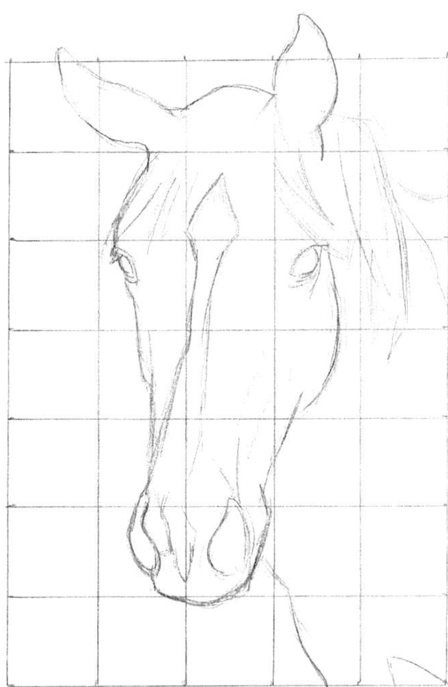

Step 1
Study the shapes you see within each square. This is what your line drawing should look like.

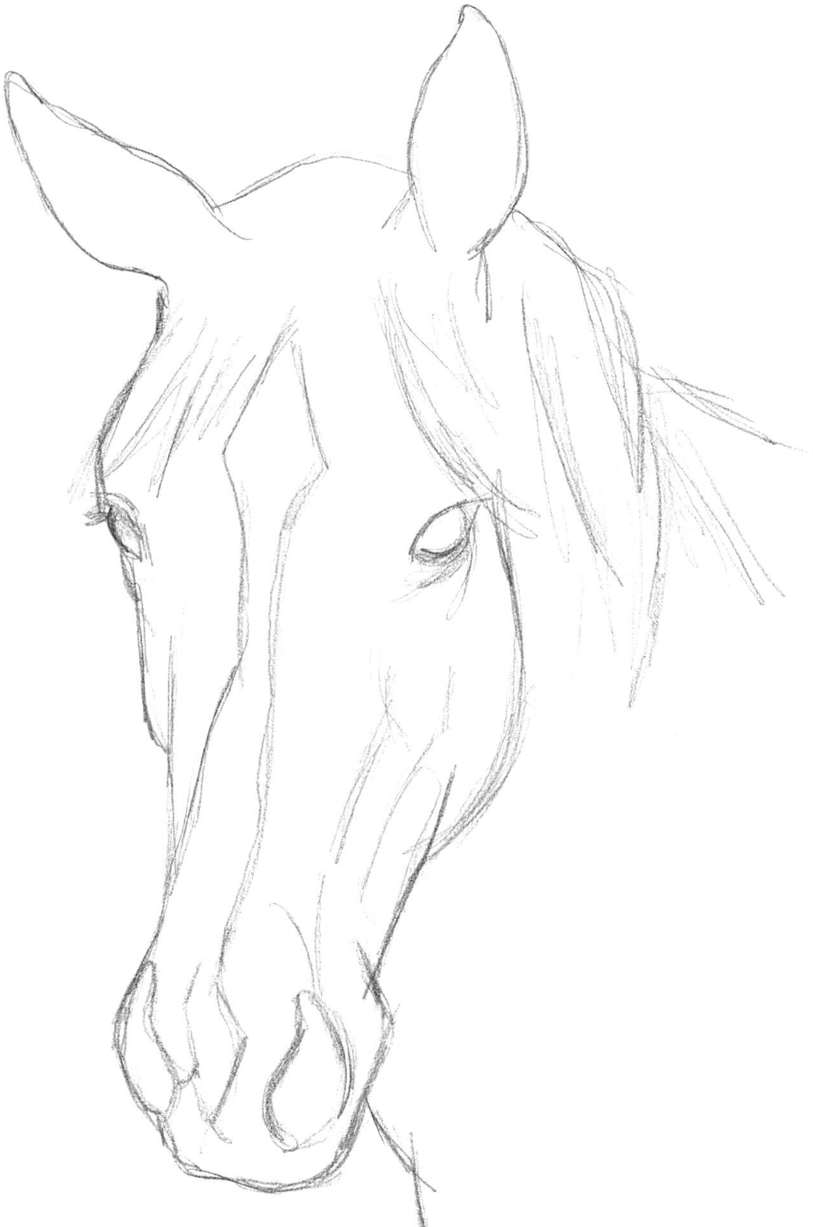

Step 2
When you are sure of the accuracy of your drawing, remove your graph lines with your kneaded eraser. Your drawing will now look like this.

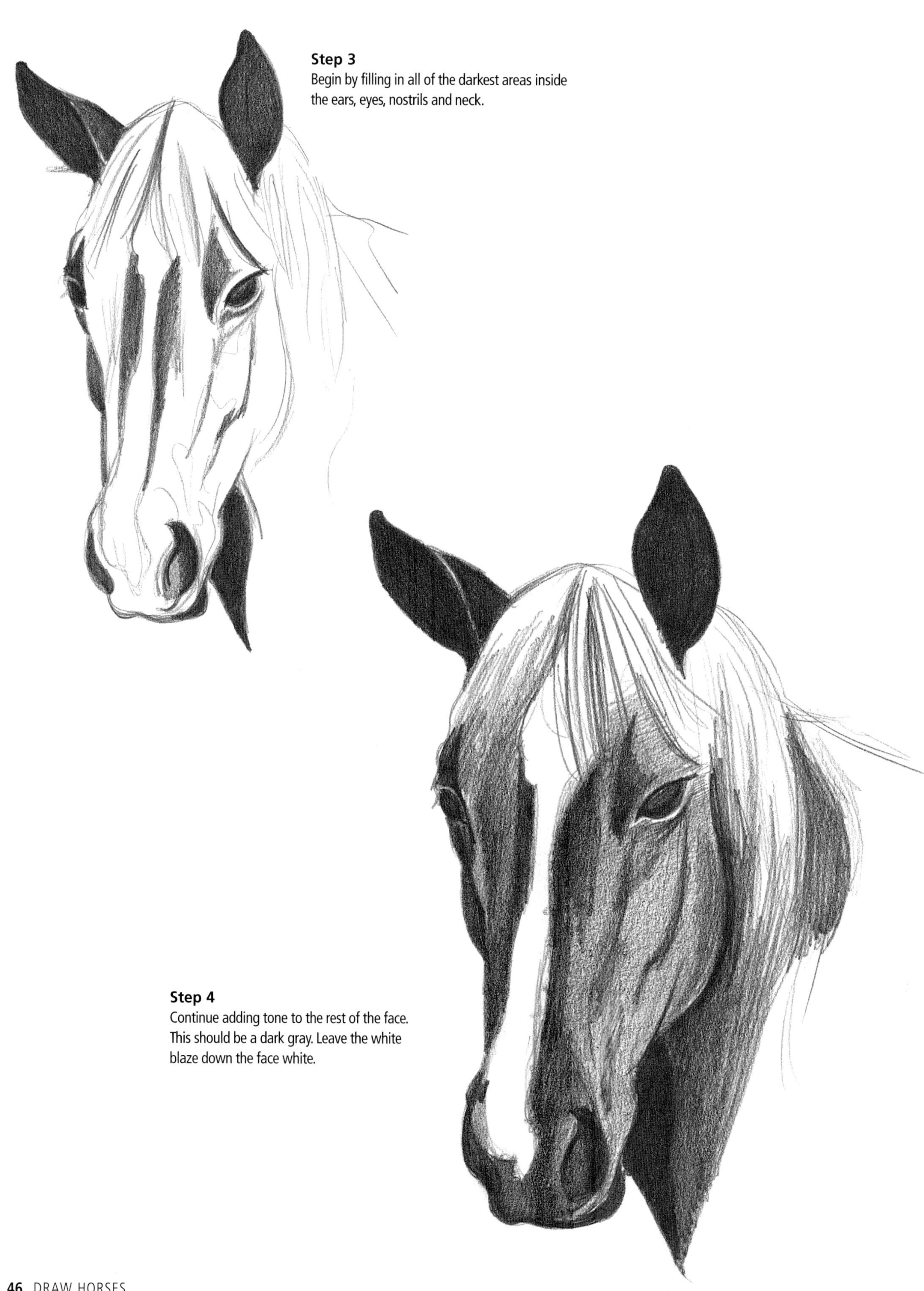

Step 3
Begin by filling in all of the darkest areas inside the ears, eyes, nostrils and neck.

Step 4
Continue adding tone to the rest of the face. This should be a dark gray. Leave the white blaze down the face white.

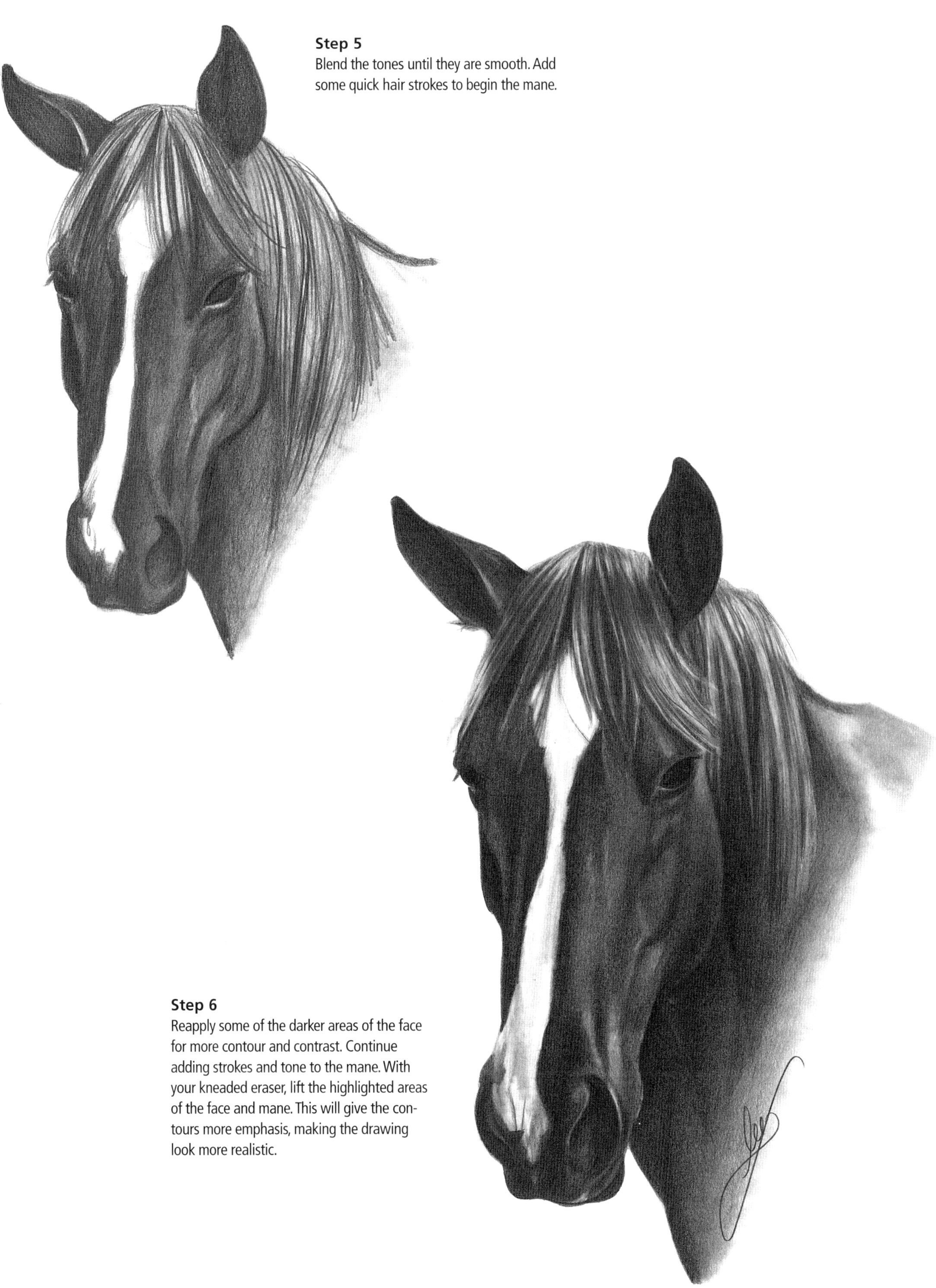

Step 5

Blend the tones until they are smooth. Add some quick hair strokes to begin the mane.

Step 6

Reapply some of the darker areas of the face for more contour and contrast. Continue adding strokes and tone to the mane. With your kneaded eraser, lift the highlighted areas of the face and mane. This will give the contours more emphasis, making the drawing look more realistic.

PROJECT 2

I chose this photo to give you practice drawing a lighter colored horse. I loved the soft gray color. It almost appeared like suede. I liked the way the long, light eyelashes of the horse showed up against its dark eyes. I also liked the contrast of the dark mane against the light colored face and neck. Because of the close-up shot, the vein of its face is also clearly seen. This is an important feature that can usually be seen in the horse's face. It should always be included to aid in the realism.

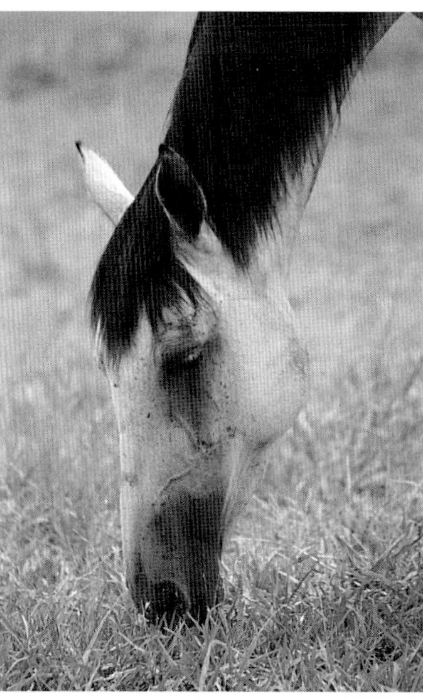

This photo will give you practice drawing a light colored horse. I like the relaxed pose, typical of a horse in the field. I had the picture copied and enlarged, and placed the graph over it.

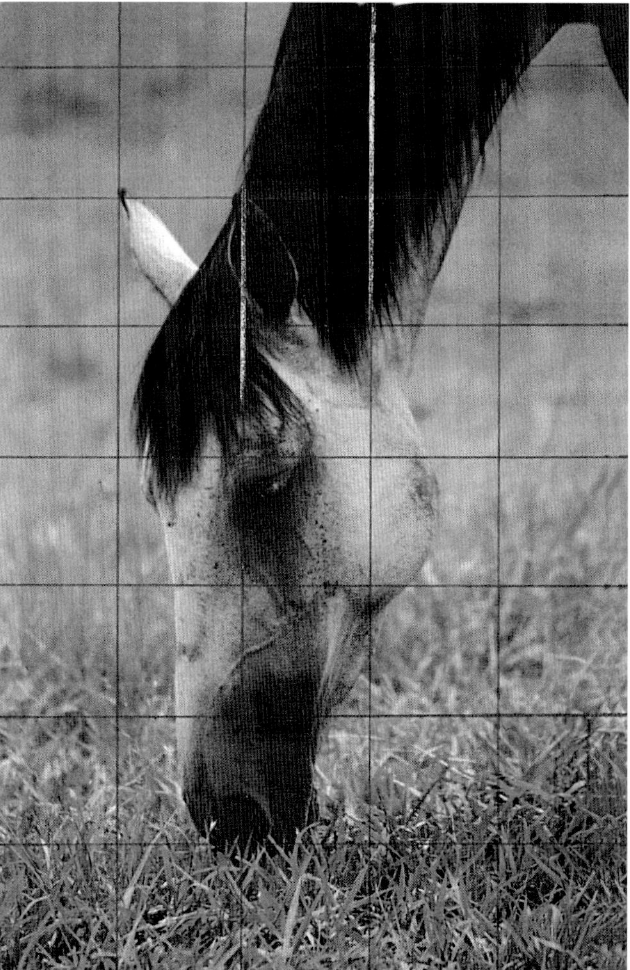

Use this graphed photo as a guide for drawing this pose.

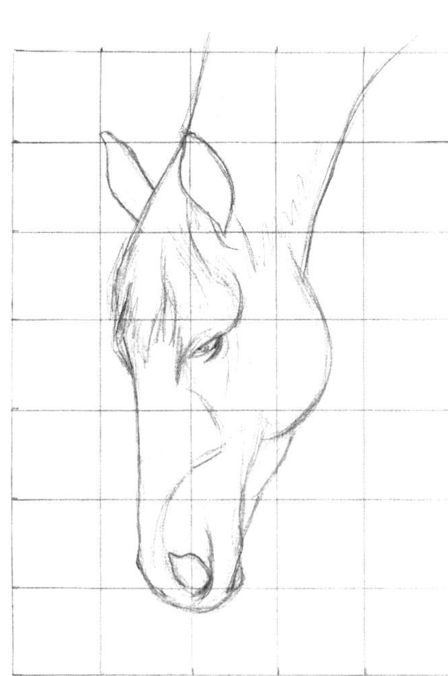

Step 1
This is what your line drawing should look like in your graph.

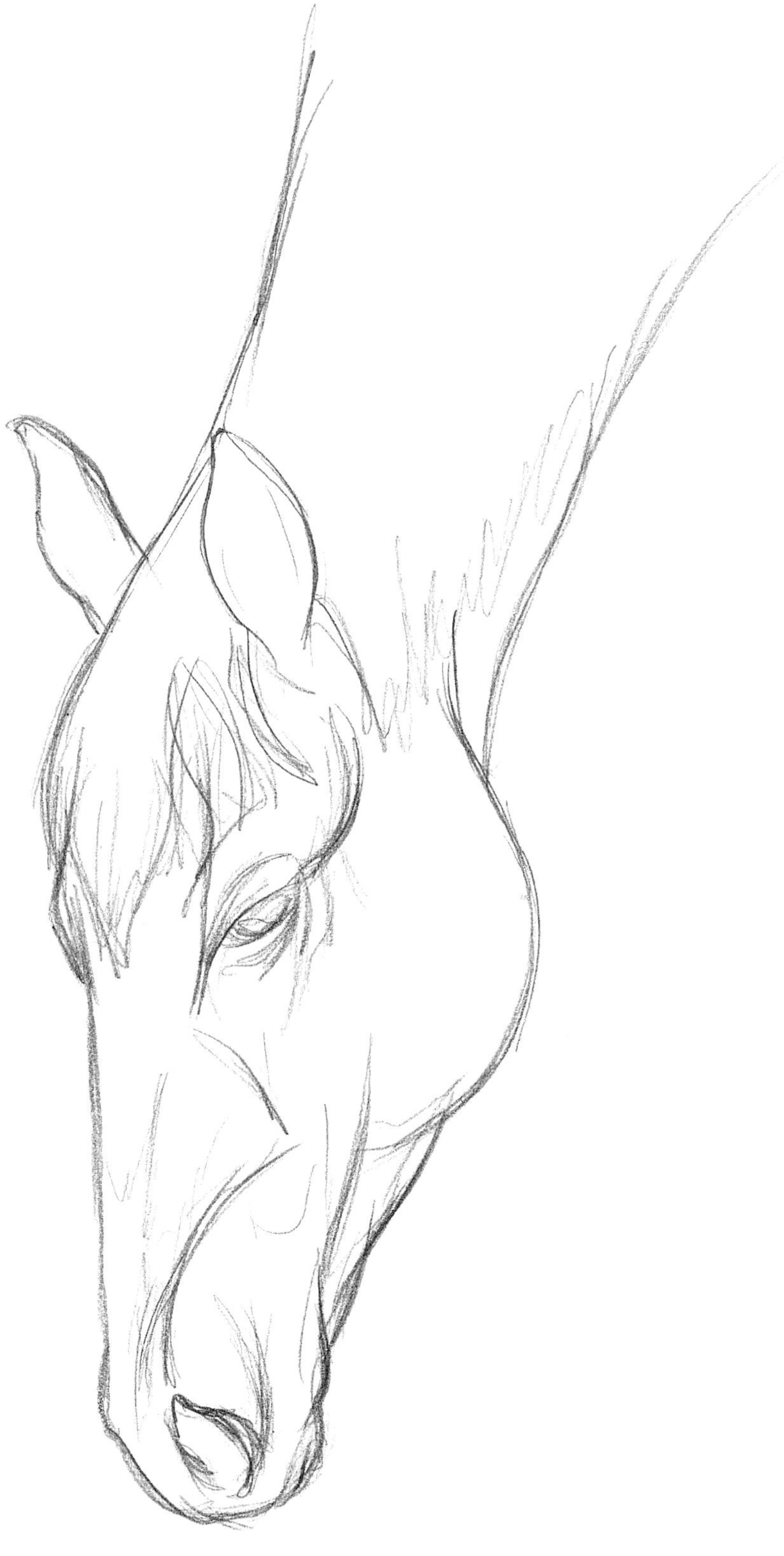

Step 2
When you are sure of the accuracy of your shapes, remove your graph lines with your kneaded eraser. Your drawing should look like this.

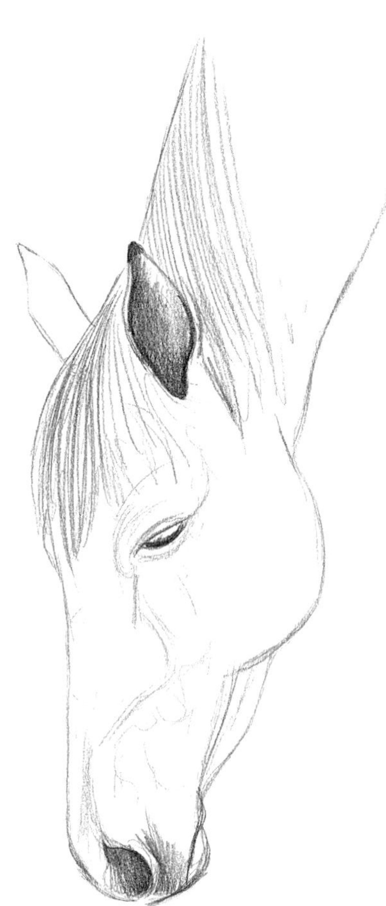

Step 3
Begin by placing in the darkest tones. These are found in the ear, the nostril and the eye. Leave the light area for the eyelashes. Add some quick strokes to begin the mane.

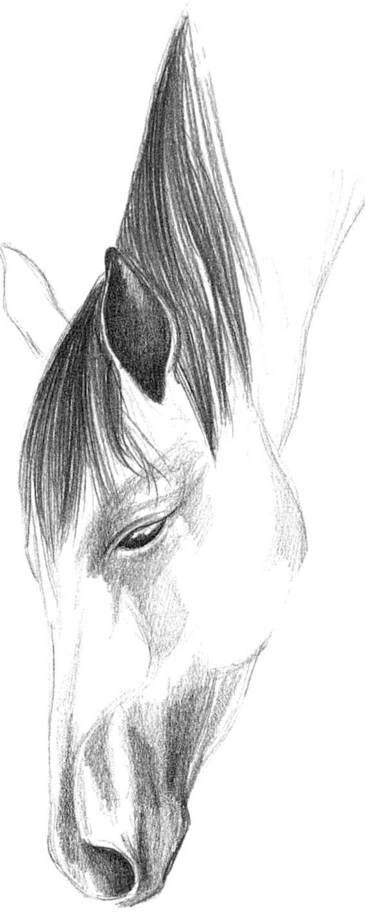

Step 4
Continue adding dark pencil strokes to the mane to fill it in. Add some medium gray tones to the face to create the facial contours.

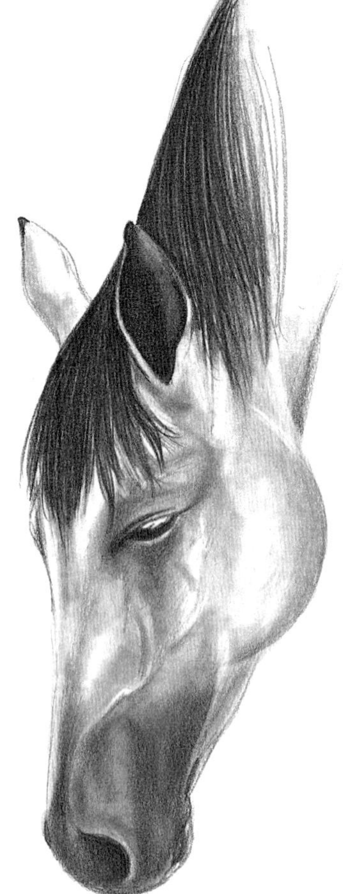

Step 5
With the tortillion, blend the tones out until smooth. Blend the mane also. Look at how the values of tone create the shape of the face. The vein running down the face, below the eye, is a very important feature. Keep it light there. Don't let it fill in.

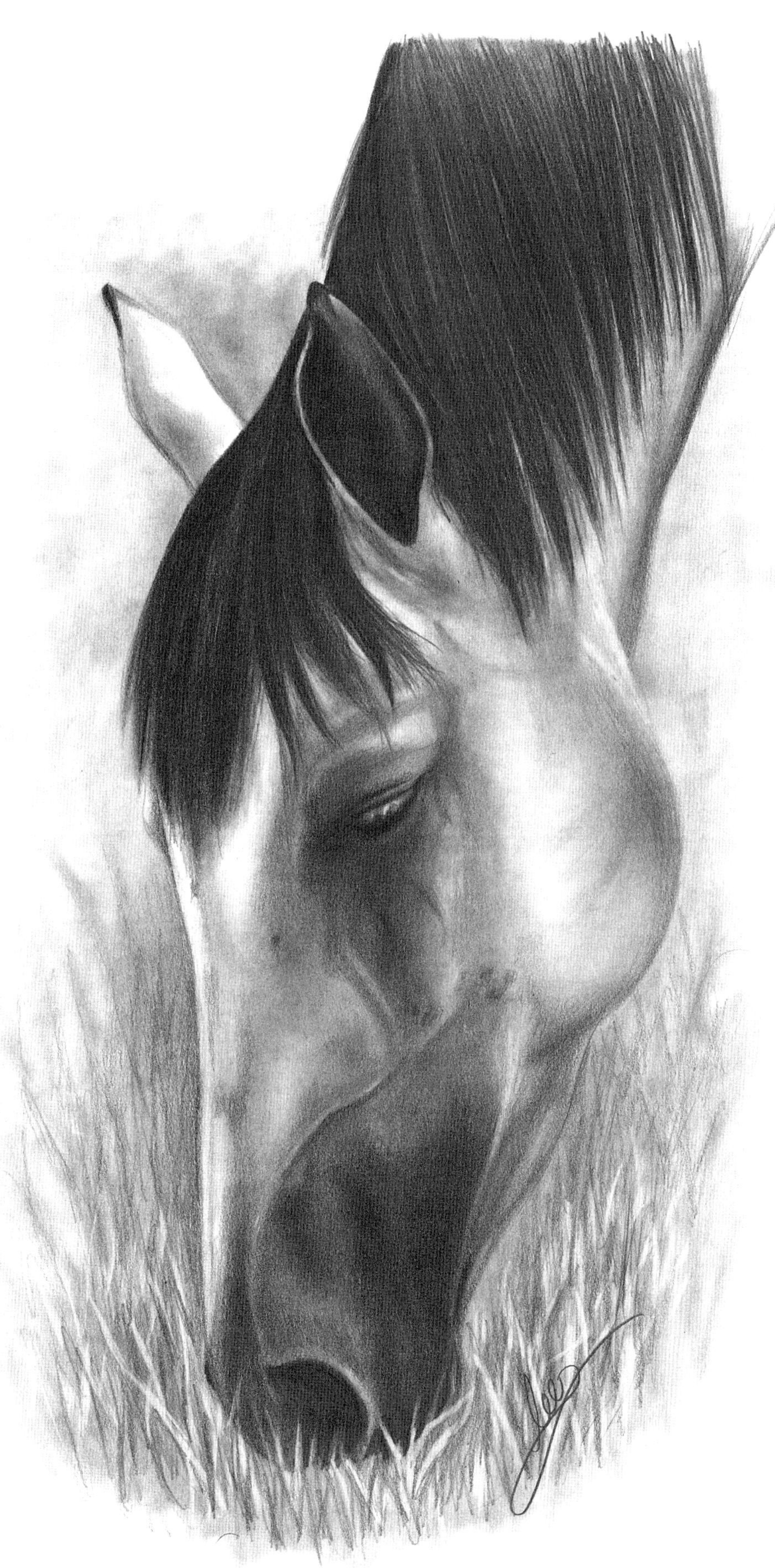

Step 6

Finish the drawing by lifting out all of the reflected light areas. Place the tone behind the horse's face to make the light edges stand out. This will make the cheek and jaw area resemble a sphere exercise. Create the illusion of grass for a realistic setting. This is done by blending tone out horizontally, to give the shadow effect. Then apply quick strokes with the pencil and the kneaded eraser to replicate the look of dark and light grass blades. The closer it is, the more detail you'll need. The background is mostly just blending, to make it recede.

PROJECT 3

This back view of the previous horse gives you a unique opportunity to see how the head appears from behind. It clearly depicts the bone structure of the jaws and muzzle. Drawing this view may be more difficult than the poses from the previous exercises. This is due to the fact that it is a pose we are not used to looking at. The shapes are not recognizable, so our brains will pump our heads full of descriptions of what a horse is supposed to look like. When drawing, just concentrate on one box at a time. See everything as inanimate shapes, and let the shapes connect like a puzzle to create the horse.

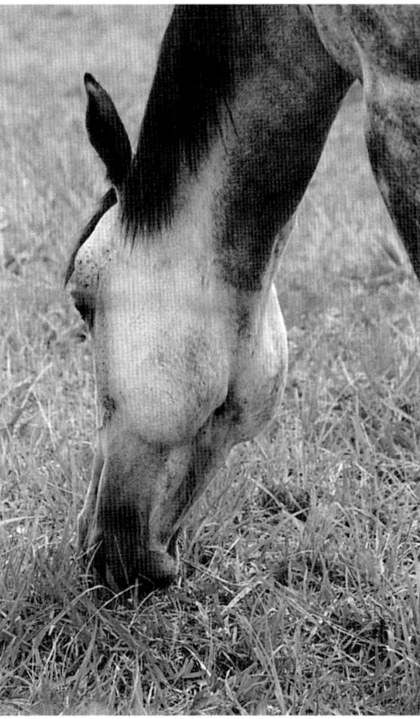

This back view of the horse's head gives you a unique pose to practice. The bone structure of the jaw and muzzle are clearly seen.

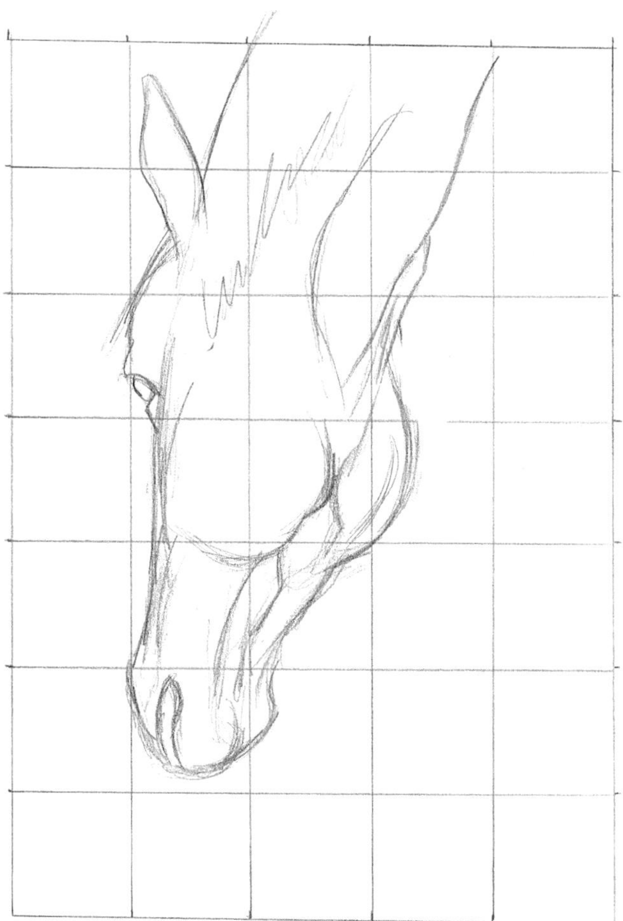

Step 1
This is what your line drawing should look like.

Step 2

When you are sure of the accuracy of your shapes, remove your graph with your kneaded eraser.

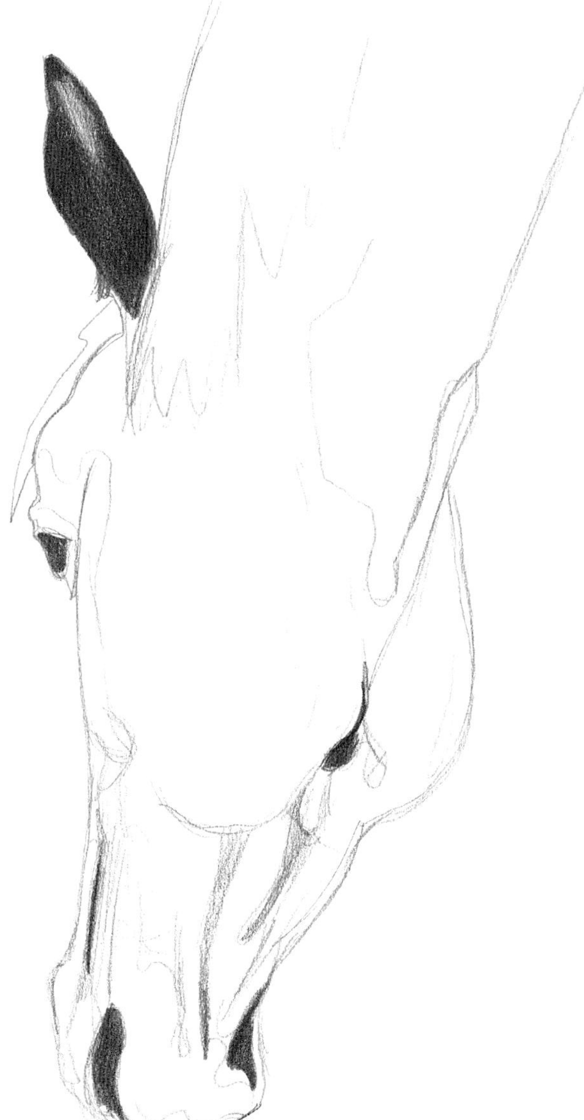

Step 3

Begin by placing in the darkest tones. These are found on the ear, in the eye, in the mouth and in the crease where the jawbones meet.

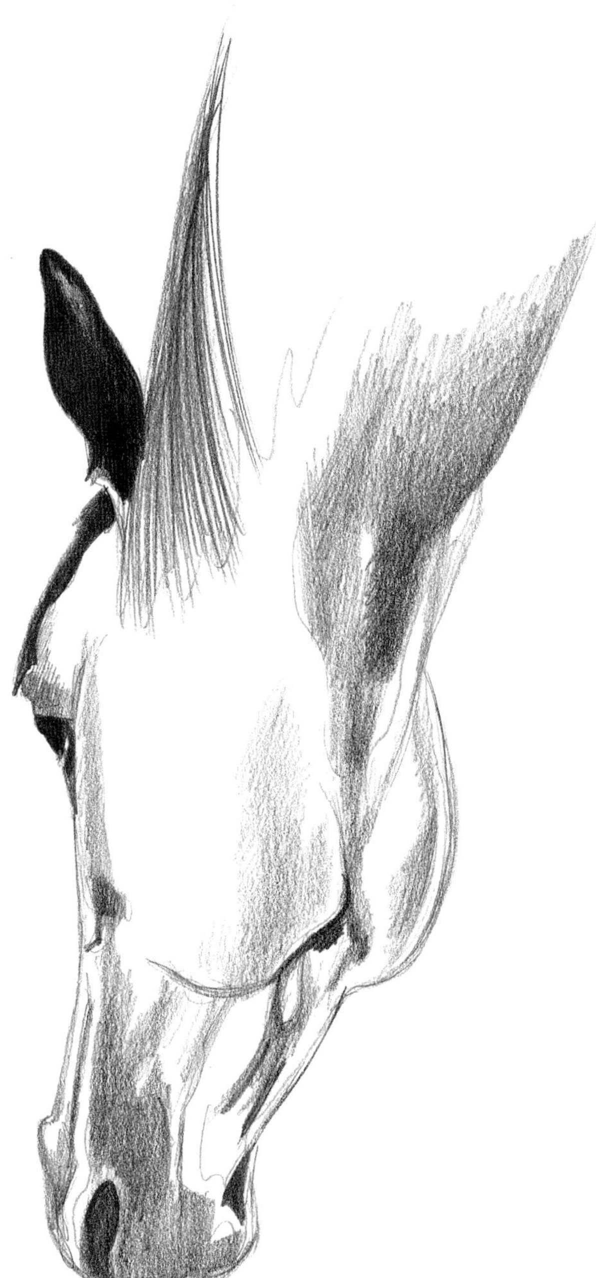

Step 4

Place medium gray tones in the neck and mouth areas, and down the front of the face. (Leave a space for the reflected light here.) Apply the shadow edges on the jaws, again leaving room for the reflected light. Apply quick strokes to begin the mane.

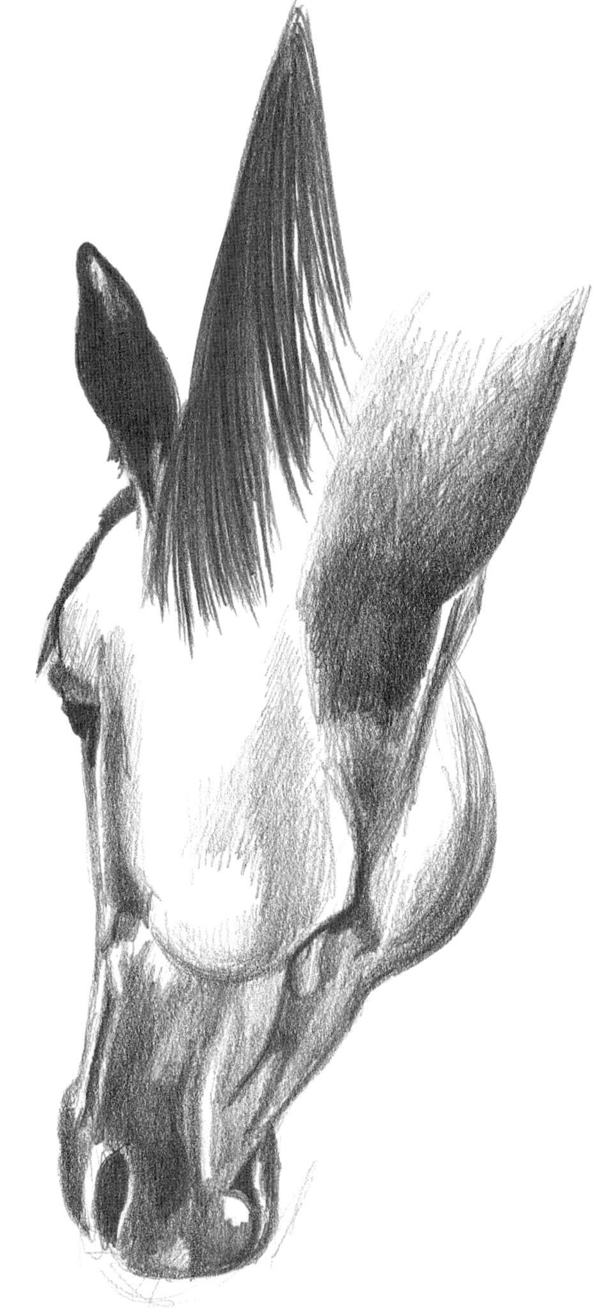

Step 5

Continue building the depth of tone. The whole right side is in shadow here. Even though this is a light horse, the tones appear dark. Continue filling the mane with layers of dark, quick strokes.

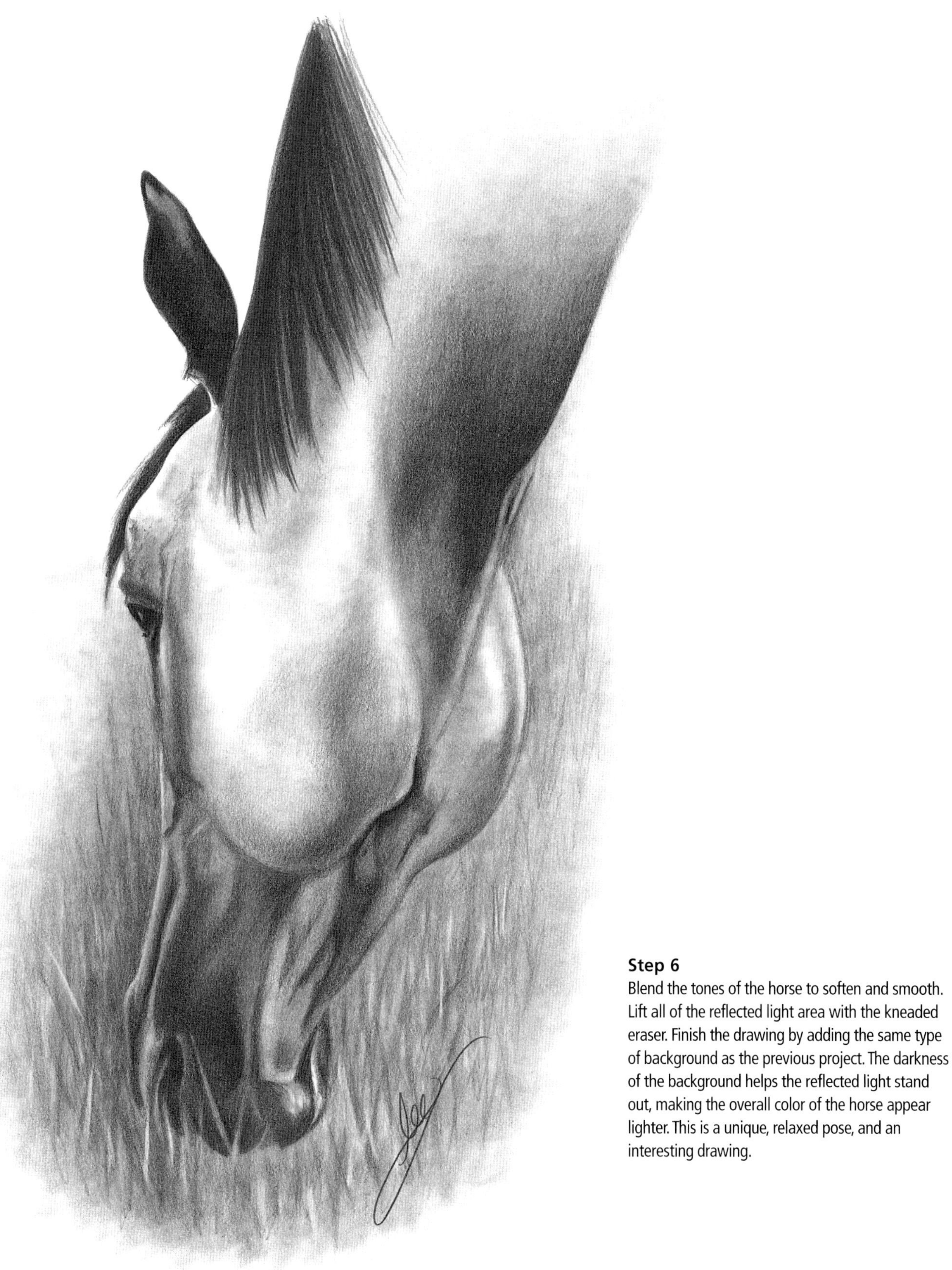

Step 6

Blend the tones of the horse to soften and smooth. Lift all of the reflected light area with the kneaded eraser. Finish the drawing by adding the same type of background as the previous project. The darkness of the background helps the reflected light stand out, making the overall color of the horse appear lighter. This is a unique, relaxed pose, and an interesting drawing.

Chapter Ten

Drawing Hooves and Legs

To draw the entire horse, it is important to know how to correctly draw the legs and the hoof area. As with the chapters before, it is imperative to see things as shapes, not as subject matter.

The hoof is very angular. It is wider in the back, to support the weight of the horse. It is narrower in the front. It slants out and down from the leg. The color of the hoof will vary from horse to horse, depending on the breed and its coloration. Remember the angles and the basic shapes as you draw. The following pages will show you how to draw the hoof correctly.

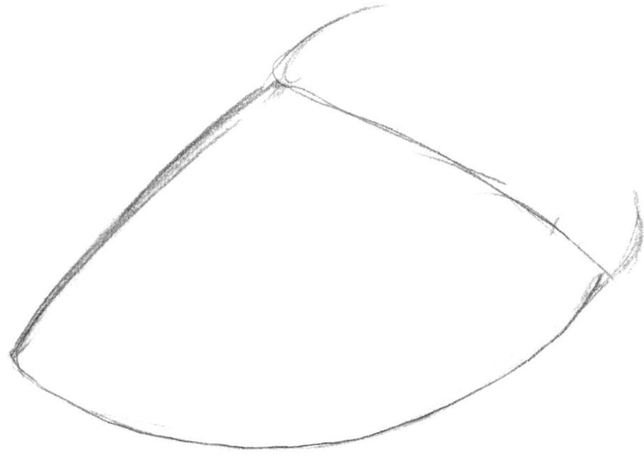

By examining the hoof as basic shapes, you can draw it more accurately. The hoof has a slant to it. It angles downward, and out from the leg.

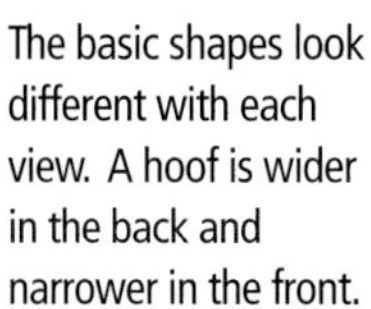

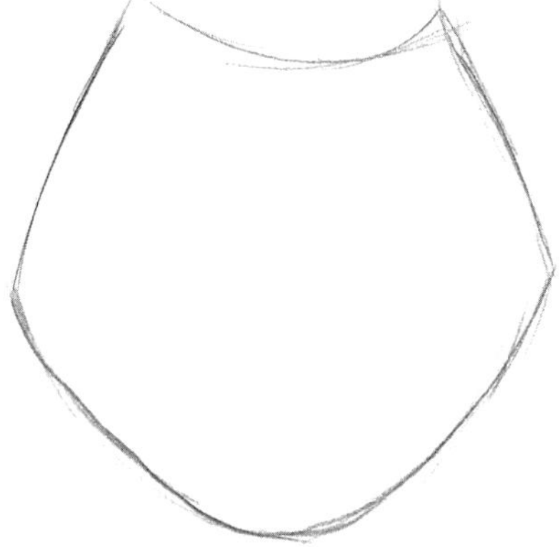

The basic shapes look different with each view. A hoof is wider in the back and narrower in the front.

A view of a horse's hoof from the front.

HOOF EXERCISES

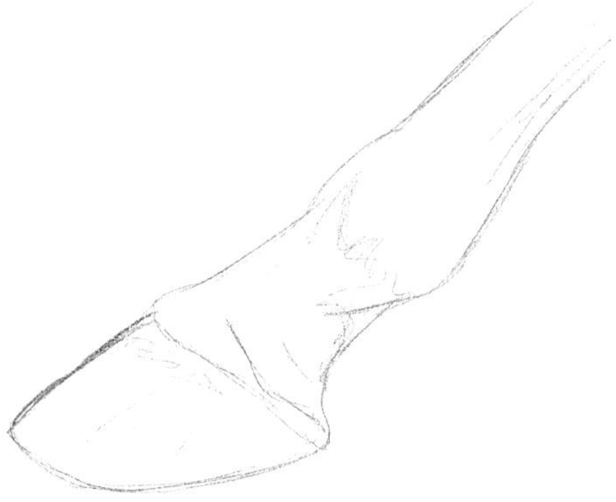

Step 1
Start with an accurate line drawing. Be careful to draw in the angles of the ankle joint and the hoof.

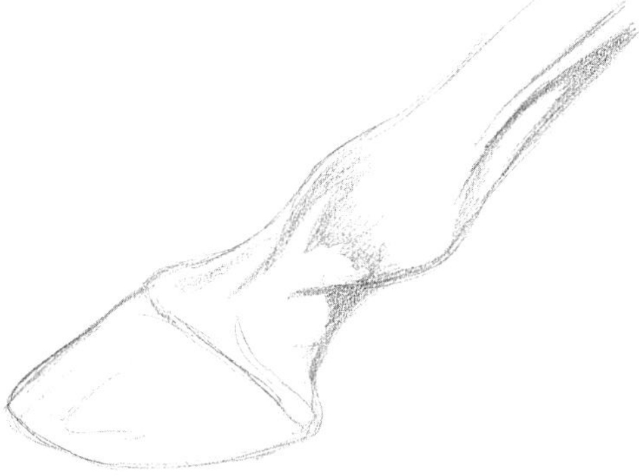

Step 2
Place in the darker tones around the ankle joint. Develop the recessed area on the leg where the tendon shows.

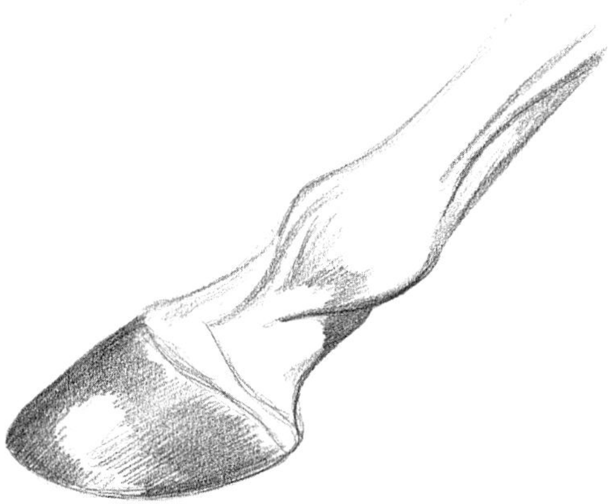

Step 3
Apply dark tones to the hoof area. Leave the highlighted area lighter.

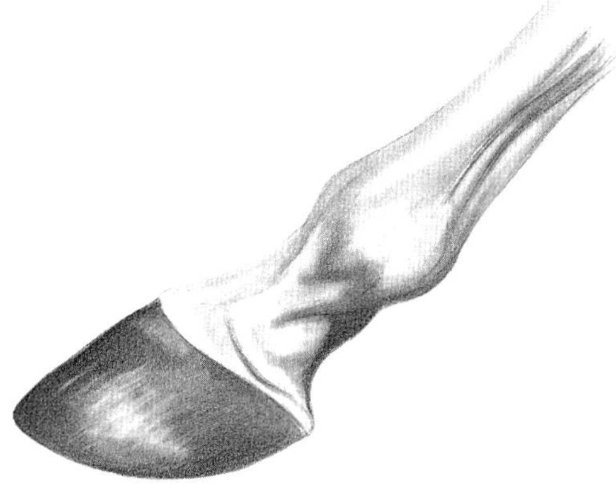

Step 4
Blend the tones to soften and smooth. Lift the highlight area on the hoof to make it look shiny. This is done with your kneaded eraser.

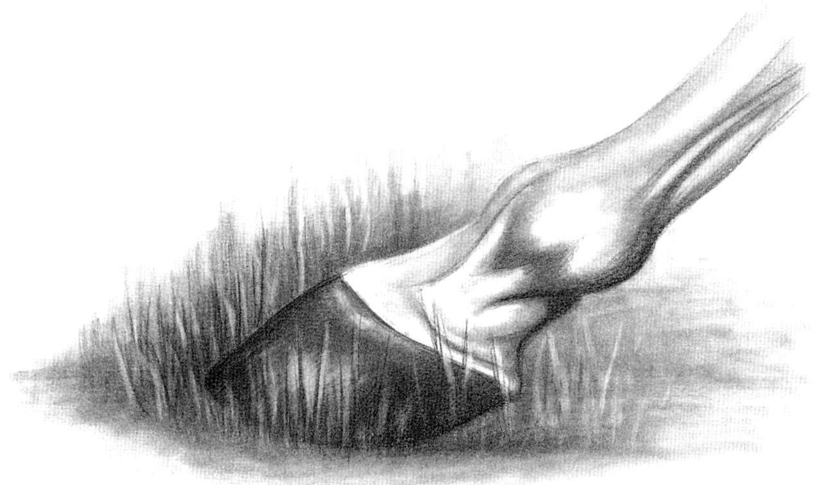

Step 5
Create the illusion of ground and grass using the same technique we used in the previous chapter. (See page 51.) This makes the horse hoof look like it is stepping on firm ground.

LEGS

The legs of a horse are more complicated than you would think. They are very detailed due to the bone structure, muscles and tendons. All of these elements are seen easily. Study the two drawings on this page carefully and you will see what I mean. The lean body structure shows the joints and the other characteristics clearly. All of these elements must be included to make the legs appear realistic. These are what gives the legs their form. Without them, the leg will appear too straight, and tubular. Look carefully for the areas of reflected light on the legs. Every raised area has light dancing off of it!

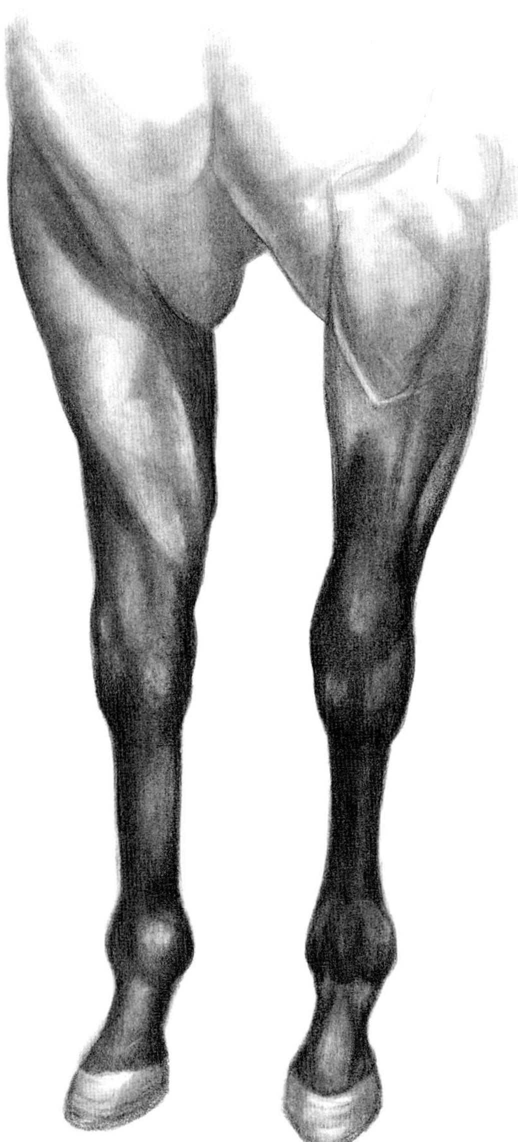

A front view of a horse's legs. Look for the muscles of the leg, as well as the joints and tendons.

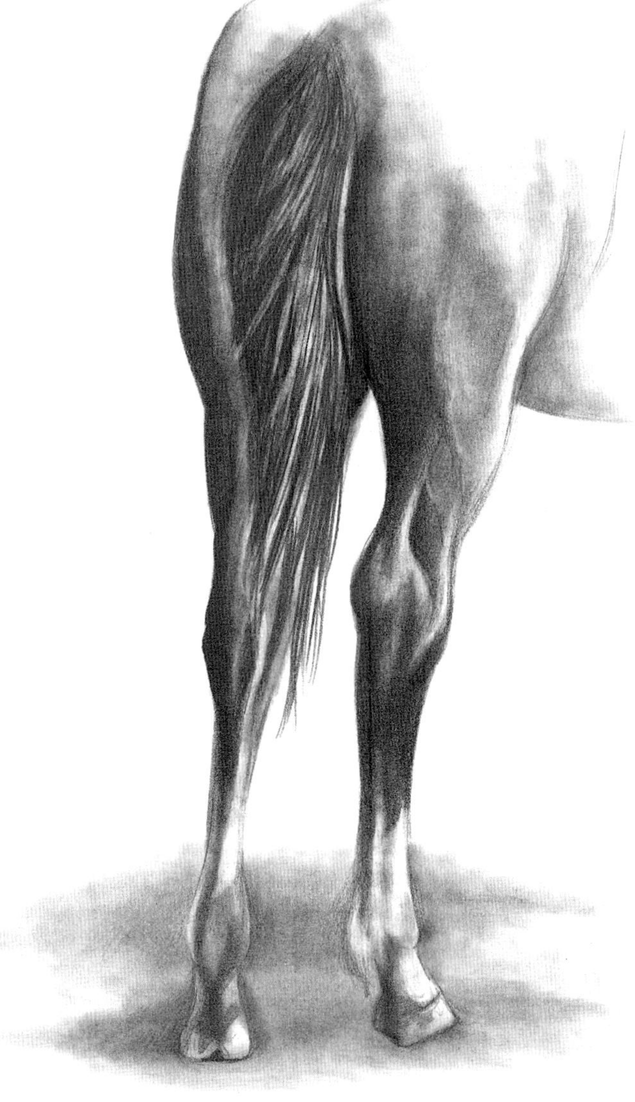

The rear view of a horse's legs. Look at the reflected light along all of the raised surfaces. Study the joints carefully. It is this type of detail that will make your work look professional.

LEG POSES

These poses show you all of the details of the leg. Look closely for the anatomical details seen in each pose. Study them carefully for muscles, joints, tendons and even the veins of the leg. All of them are extremely important to your work. Look at the basic shapes that make up the legs and the hooves.

You can see how each view offers you a different set of details to look for. By studying the horse in as many poses as possible, you will learn to see these details more easily. I studied many pictures, books and photographs to teach myself what to look for when drawing. I also studied as many live horses as I could find, just to become more familiar with them. This is what a good artist must do. Although I have been around horses my whole life, I didn't really see them until I started drawing them.

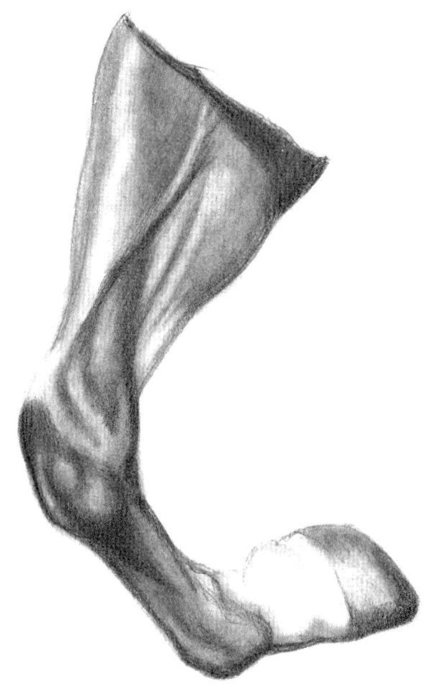

The front leg of a horse, as viewed from the side. The muscles are easily seen from this view, as well as the veins and tendons.

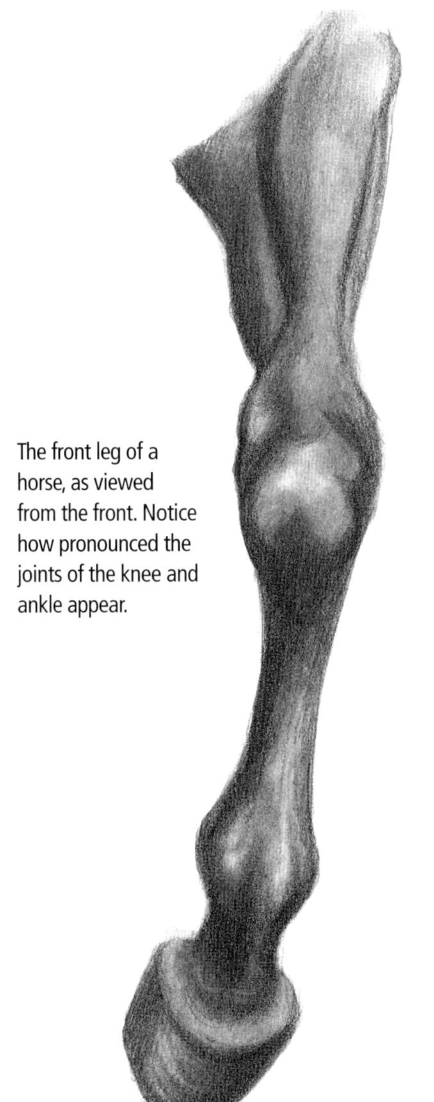

The front leg of a horse, as viewed from the front. Notice how pronounced the joints of the knee and ankle appear.

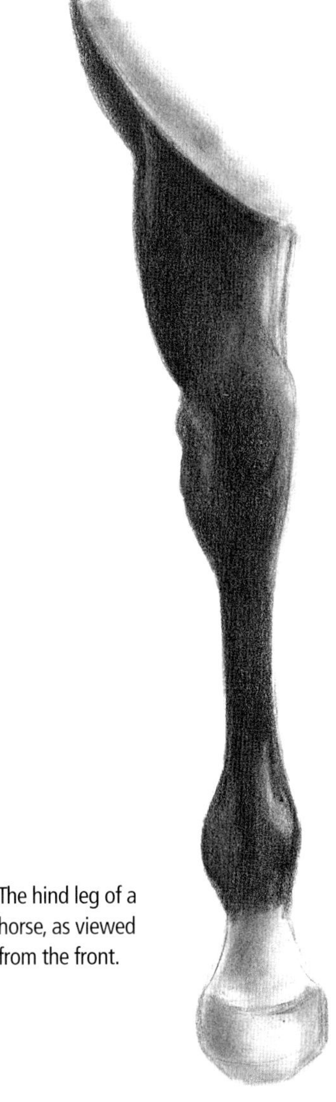

The hind leg of a horse, as viewed from the front.

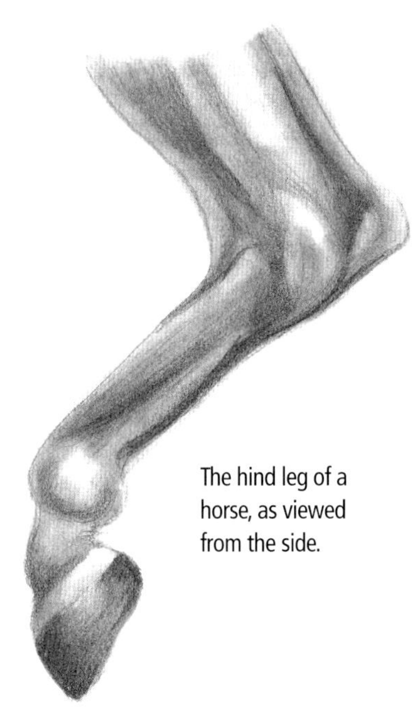

The hind leg of a horse, as viewed from the side.

Chapter Eleven

Drawing the Whole Horse

We are now ready to draw the horse in its entirety. The photograph shown here is a good place to start. The casual walking and front view make this a pleasing pose. More importantly, it is a good position to observe the effects of foreshortening. This is a term that applies to any long object that is projecting forward. What happens in this case is that the length of the horse is distorted due to perspective. What you see is the front of the horse clearly, while the midsection seems short. Look at the examples below of a long cylinder. From this view, you see the front, but the middle is condensed.

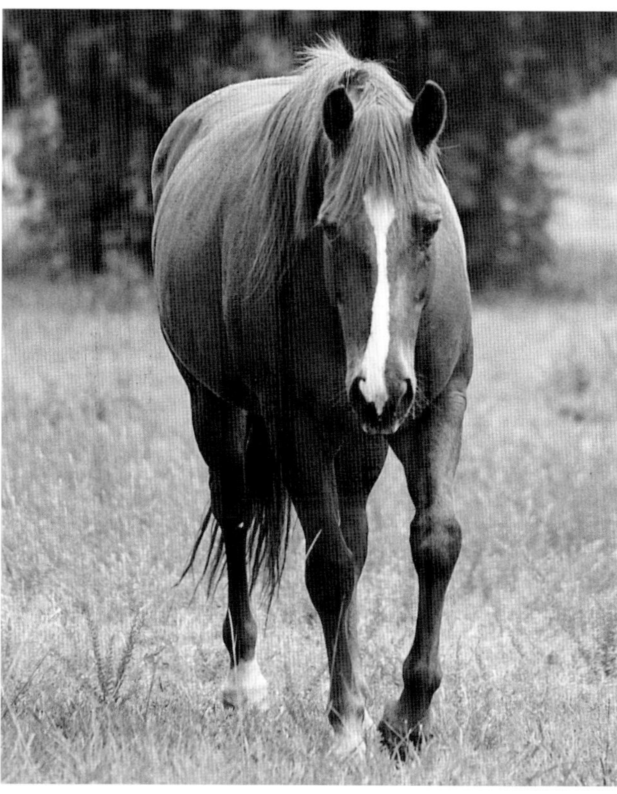

Use this photo of a horse walking for your drawing. Study the effects of "foreshortening" in this pose.

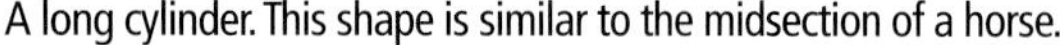

A long cylinder. This shape is similar to the midsection of a horse.

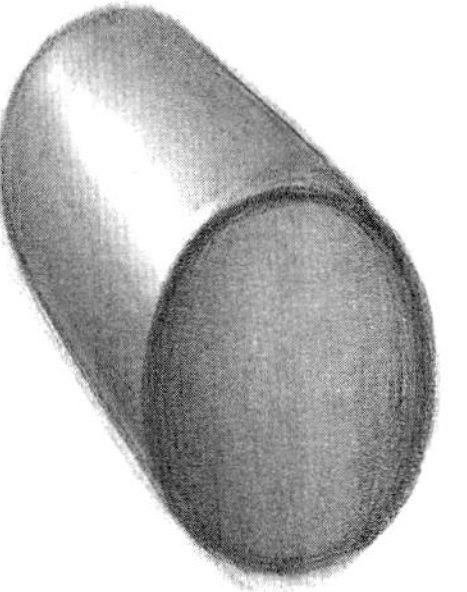

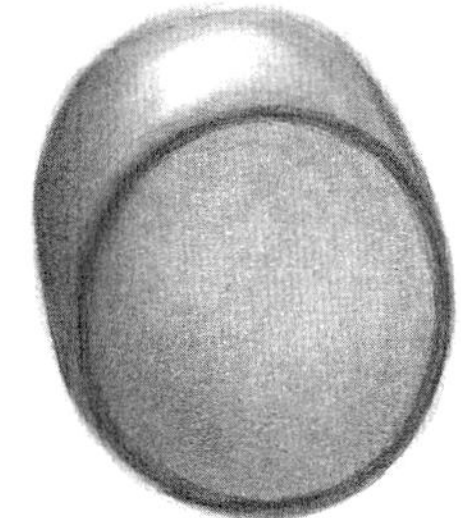

When the cylinder is turned toward you, the length appears shorter. The distance is changed due to perspective.

FRONT VIEW

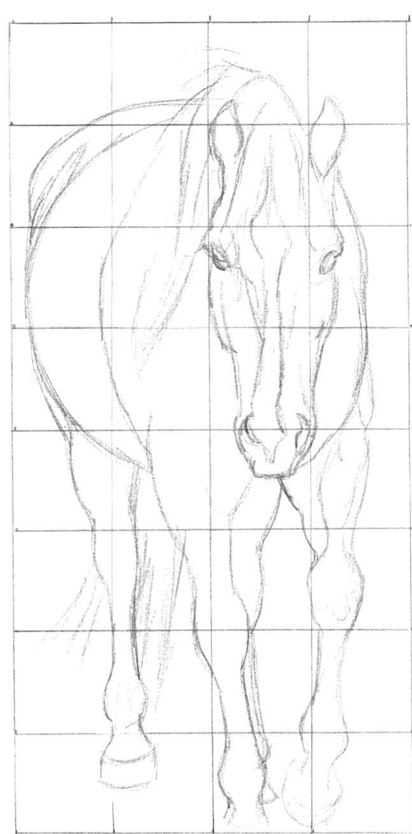

Step 1
An accurate line drawing inside a graph. Check each square for accuracy in your work.

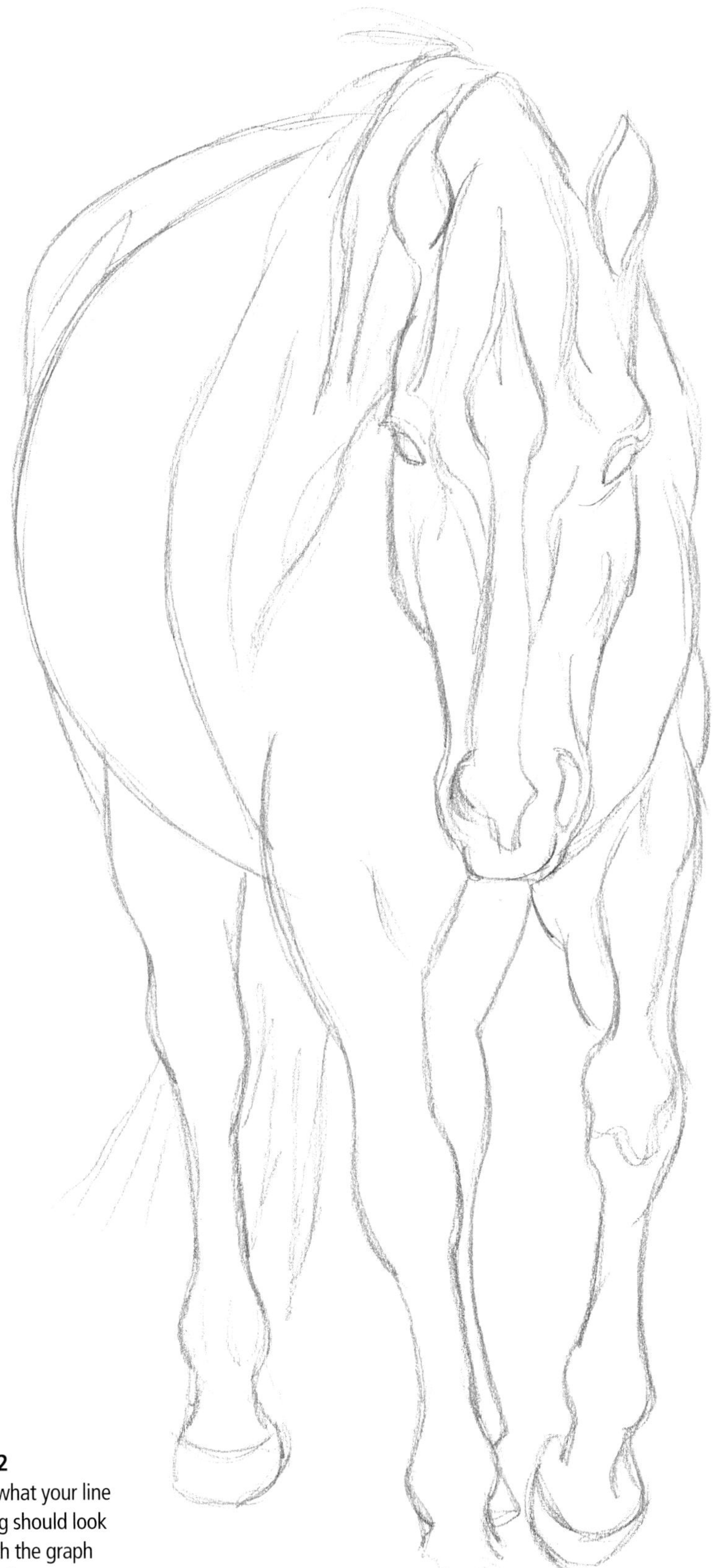

Step 2
This is what your line drawing should look like with the graph removed.

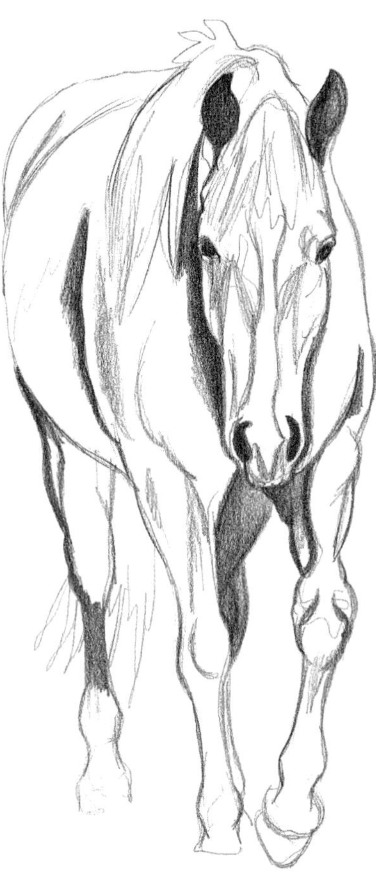

Step 3
Always begin a drawing by placing the darkest areas in first. Look for all of the shadow areas and overlapping surfaces.

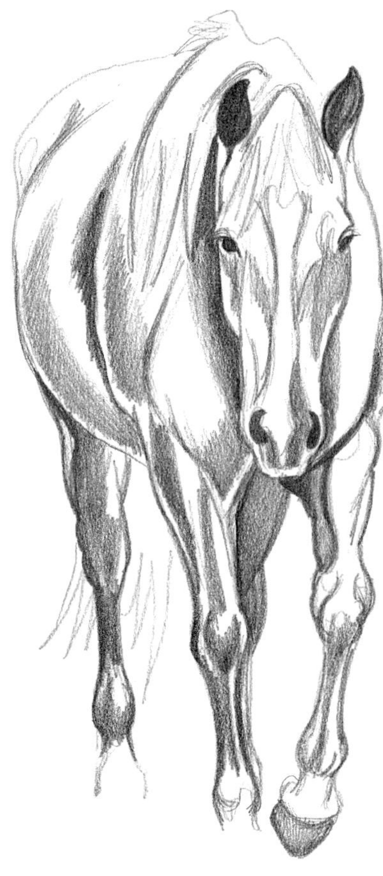

Step 4
Place in the midtones to begin creating the contours of the body. Always look for the elements of the sphere in rounded areas. The horse's belly is a good example in this pose. Remember to leave room for the reflected light.

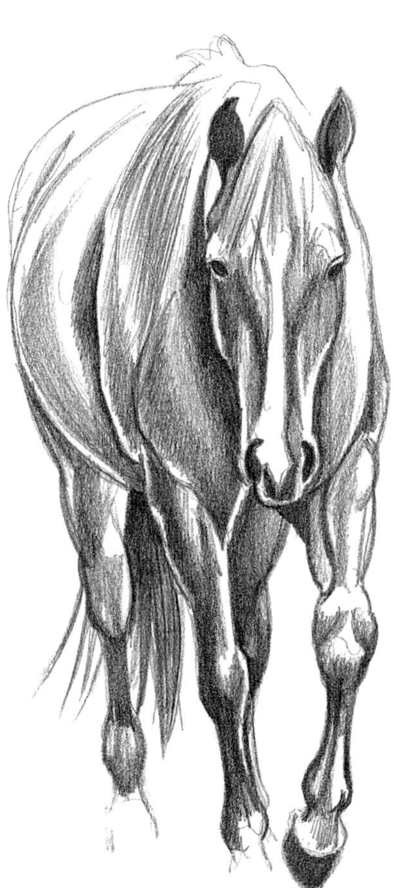

Step 5
Continue adding tones to not only create the shapes, but to replicate the color of the horse. Use quick pencil lines to begin the layers of the mane.

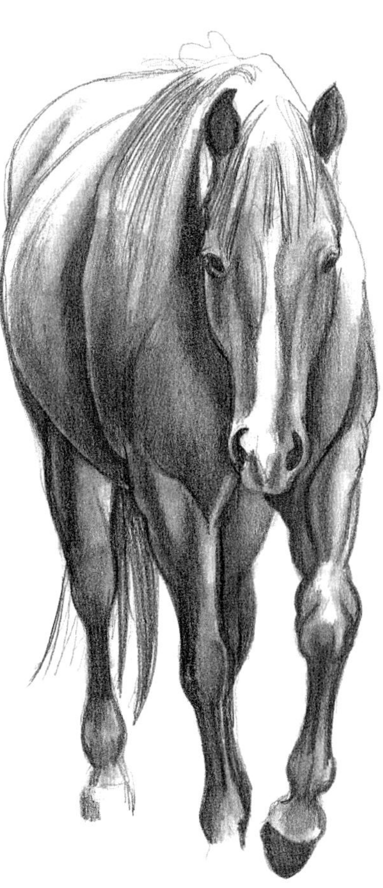

Step 6
Use a tortillion to softly blend the tones for a smoother look.

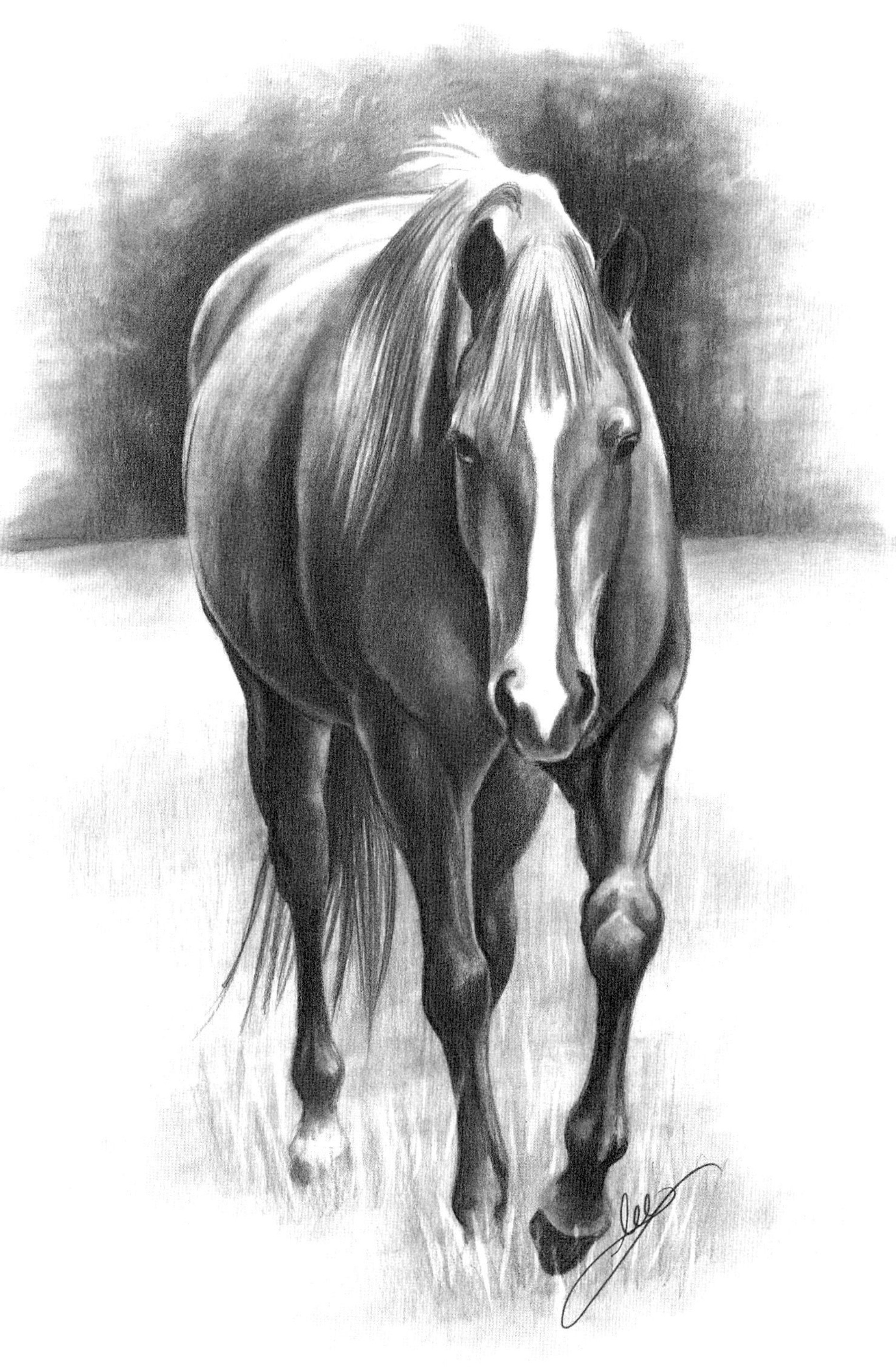

Step 7

The finished product. To finish the horse, I used the kneaded eraser to lift all of the highlight areas. This makes the light appear more realistic, and not "left out" or drawn around.

By placing a background in this drawing, not only have I created the illusion of scenery, I have given the light area along the back of the horse something to contrast against. This is so important when drawing. Always remember to eliminate outlining by creating edges instead.

To create the illusion of trees in the background, I first drew in what is called a horizon line. This gives you the feeling of distance. I then drew in vertical lines to suggest the tree trunks. I added some dark patches of tone with my pencil and scrubbed them in with a dirty tortillion. To give it more depth, I dabbed out some light areas to create the layered look of foliage

I created the look of the ground by rubbing in some areas of lighter tone using a horizontal pattern. This also gives the impression of distance. I created the look of grass using quick, vertical pencil lines, the same technique I use for drawing hair. I also lifted light strokes out with the kneaded eraser for the look of light colored grass.

BACK VIEW

This is another good pose for drawing the entire horse. This grazing stance is a typical position seen of horses in a field. I like it for the relaxed, calm mood it suggests.

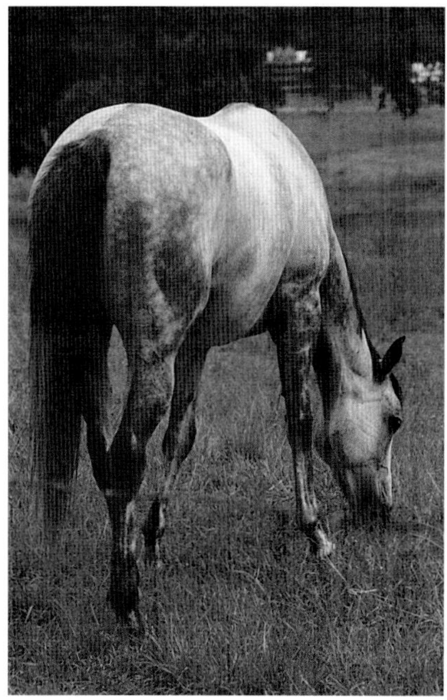

A back view of a horse. Use this photo for your drawing. This makes for a very calm, relaxed pose.

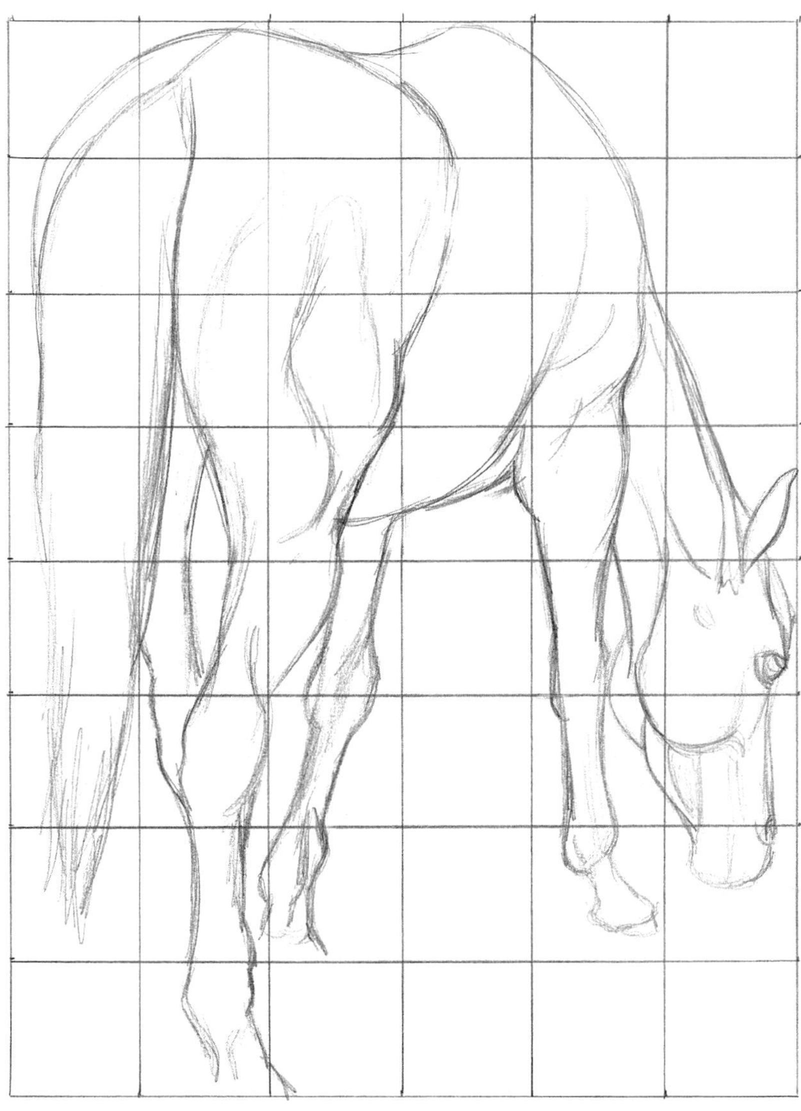

Step 1
An accurate line drawing inside a graph. Study these shapes carefully. This is what your work should look like.

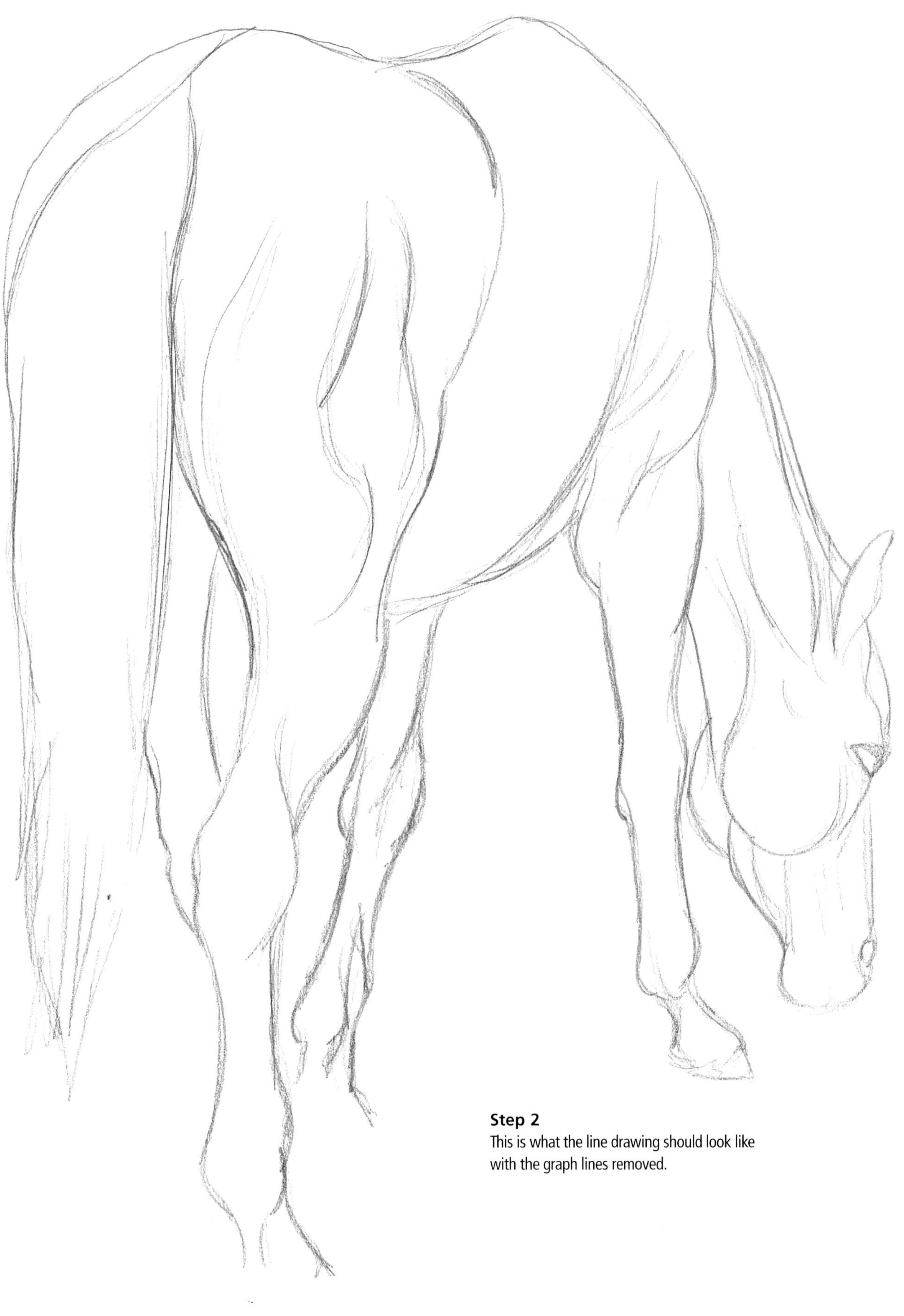

Step 2
This is what the line drawing should look like with the graph lines removed.

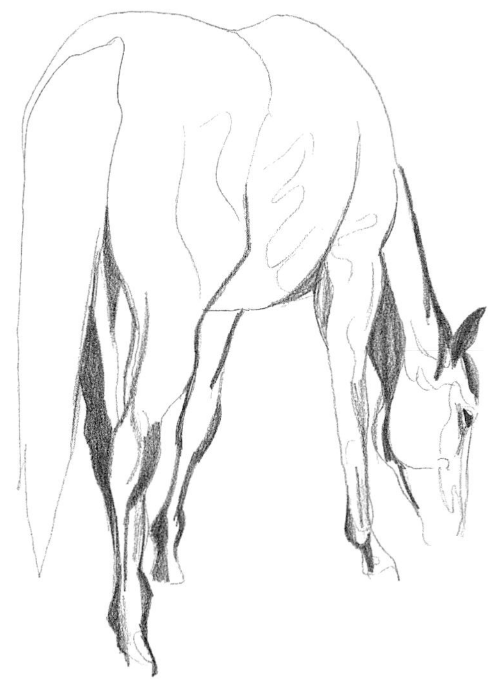

Step 3
Begin by placing the darkest tones in first. These can be found in all of the shadow areas.

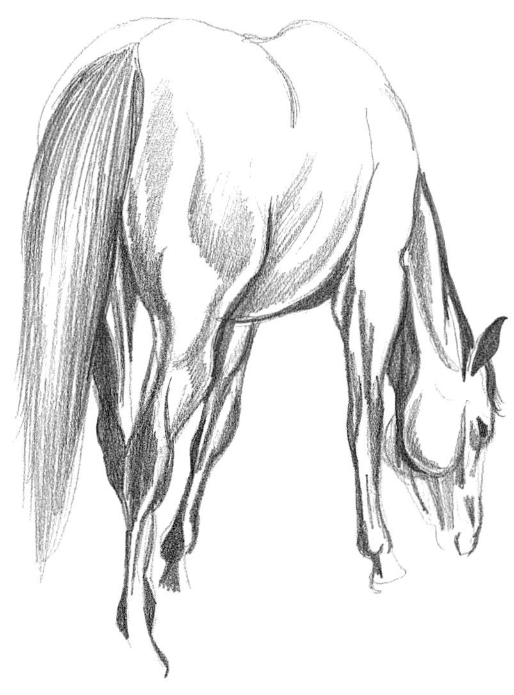

Step 4
Place the midtones for the contours of the body. Since this horse is so much lighter than the one for the previous project, it requires less tone. Also, begin the layering of pencil lines to build the tail.

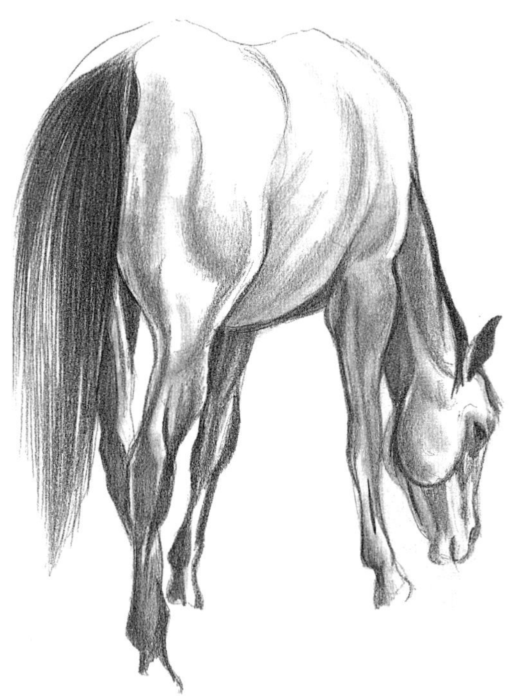

Step 5
Continue adding to the layers of the tail, until it appears dark. Leave the highlighted area lighter. With a tortillion, gently soften the tone of the body. Do not carry the tone all the way up to the top though. This horse has a strong full light area.

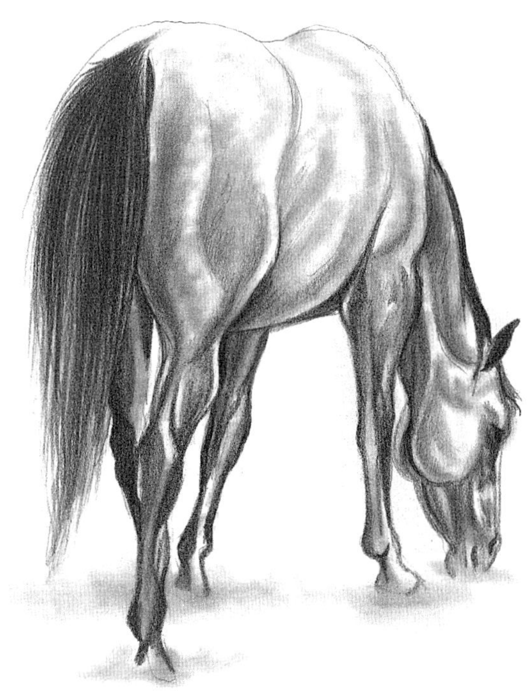

Step 6
Blend out the tail. Continue more blending in the body. Look at how I created the "Dapple Gray" effect using spotty, circular motions with the tortillion.

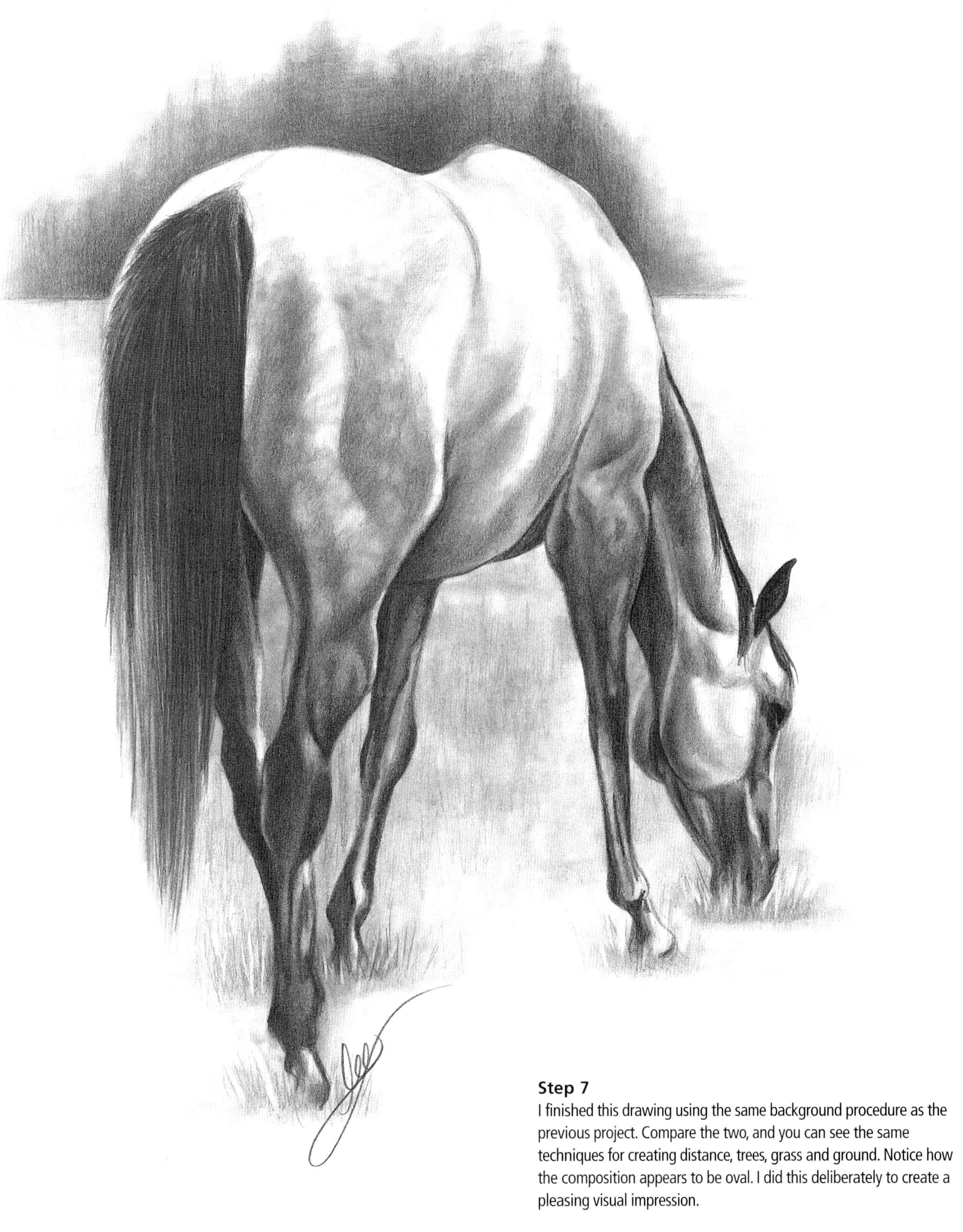

Step 7

I finished this drawing using the same background procedure as the previous project. Compare the two, and you can see the same techniques for creating distance, trees, grass and ground. Notice how the composition appears to be oval. I did this deliberately to create a pleasing visual impression.

LAYING DOWN

When drawing horses, it is also fun to draw the more unusual poses. This pose is a cute example. The curled up position of this colt makes his body seem very rounded.

If you look closely, the sphere exercise and the five elements of shading can be seen in the rounded shape of the belly. Look for the reflected light along the belly and the edge of the leg, where these two surfaces touch the ground and the shadow area. Without the reflected light, theses areas would run together.

By breaking this pose into basic shapes, you can see how to simplify the shapes, making it easier to draw. Place a graph over this drawing and practice your skills.

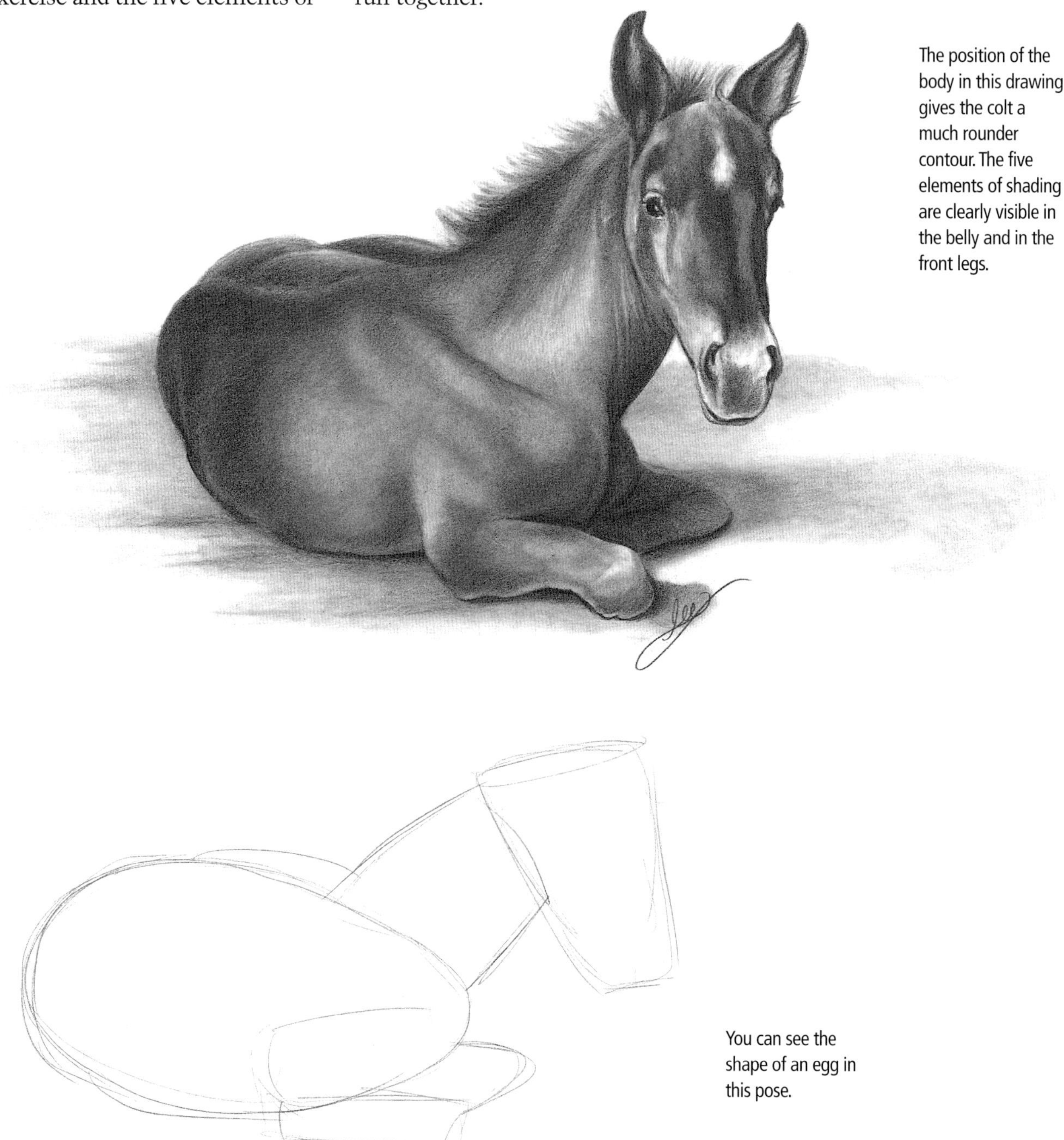

The position of the body in this drawing gives the colt a much rounder contour. The five elements of shading are clearly visible in the belly and in the front legs.

You can see the shape of an egg in this pose.

ON THE SIDE

This sleeping pose is very different from the typical poses we are used to looking at. This perspective completely changes the way the horse's features appear. Look at how the spine of the horse indents, creating a line that divides the body right down the middle. The body is very symmetrical.

By placing the blended tone around the horse, I created the illusion of foreground and background. This tone makes the light edges of the horse stand out without having to outline them.

The basic shapes of this pose are quite different from the previous drawing. Instead of the egg shape, you can see more of a cylinder.

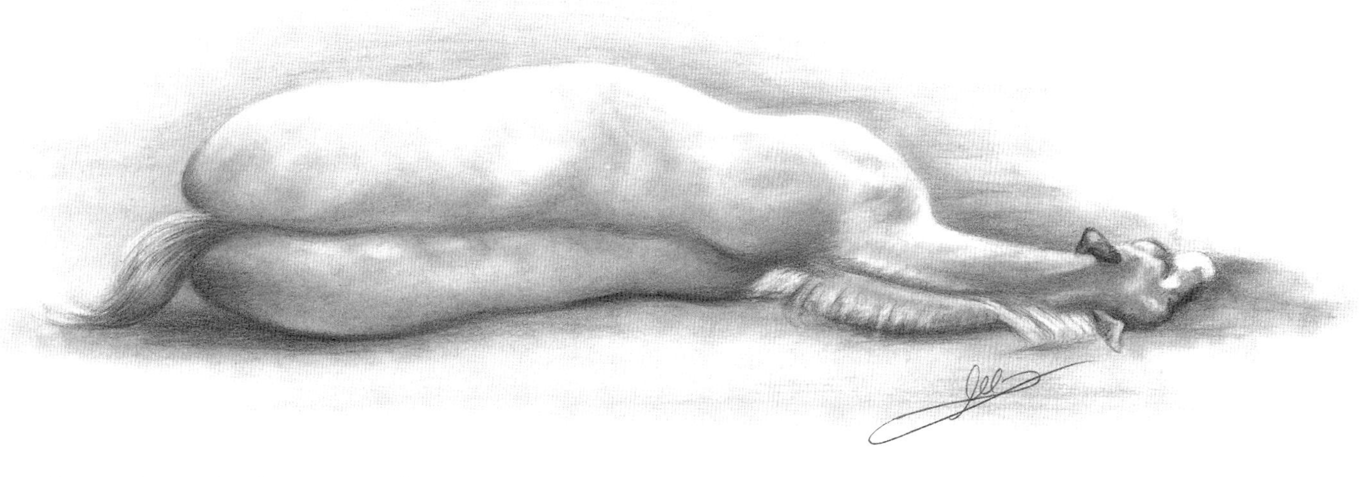

This unusual perspective allows you to see the body from the top. Look at how the spine divides the back of the colt down the middle.

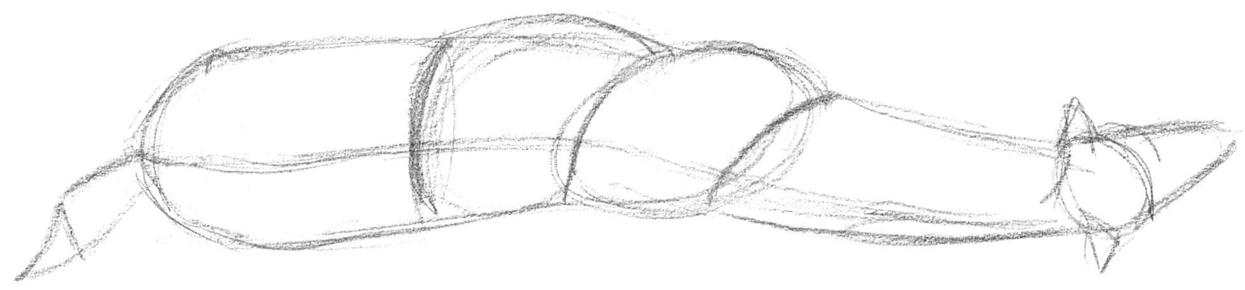

When broken down into basic shapes, you see the cylinder as its foundation, rather than the egg shape like before.

Chapter Twelve

Youngsters

Not all horses are created equal. The age of a horse plays an important factor in its appearance. Look at how long the legs of a young horse look compared to its body—they seem less muscular. The body of an older horse is heavier and filled out. It appears more balanced. The small one seems a little unsure on its feet. Look at the images on this page, and the comparisons and differences are easy to see.

When drawing this, I had to be careful with the edges. Even though we have two subjects overlapping, you will see no outlining in my drawing. I used shading to separate the surfaces. By placing strong shadows underneath them, there becomes a strong sense of the light source coming from above. The horizontal blending I used in the foreground and background helps make the ground look solid.

Age makes a difference in the shape of the face as well. Study the difference in these heads. The younger horse has much narrower features than the older one. The jaw line is much less developed and round. The mane is also shorter.

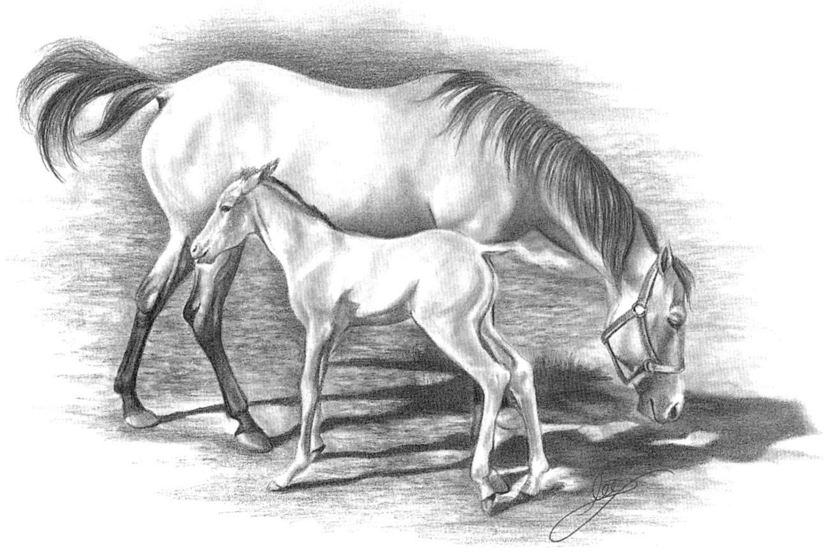

Here is a youngster with its mother. This pose makes the differences between a young horse and an adult very obvious. Notice the use of blending and edges, as opposed to outlines in this drawing. I used tones to separate the subjects.

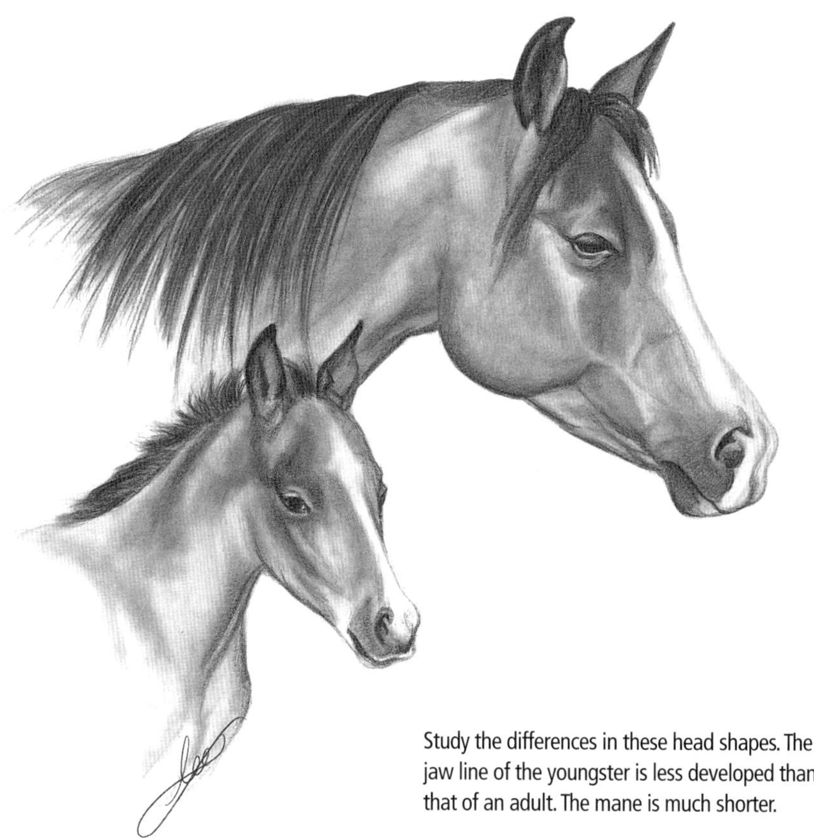

Study the differences in these head shapes. The jaw line of the youngster is less developed than that of an adult. The mane is much shorter.

Looking at these three, you can clearly see their youth. The first one is much younger than the other two. Its legs look very long, knobby and a bit wobbly. When standing, it has its legs spread out for balance. This is a good example of foreshortening, as we covered in the previous chapter. Look at how the front of the colt can be seen as well as the sides of the rump. Everything in between is blocked from view, and the distance and length of the back cannot be seen.

The second drawing shows how the body begins to fill out with age. The face still looks less defined in the jaw area than an adult however, and the legs still appear tall for the body.

Finally, this happy colt is frolicking in the sunshine. The cute pose makes the animal appear happy and frisky. By placing the shadow underneath, it helped create the feeling of movement. Most of this drawing was done with smooth blending with a tortillion, due to its even coloration.

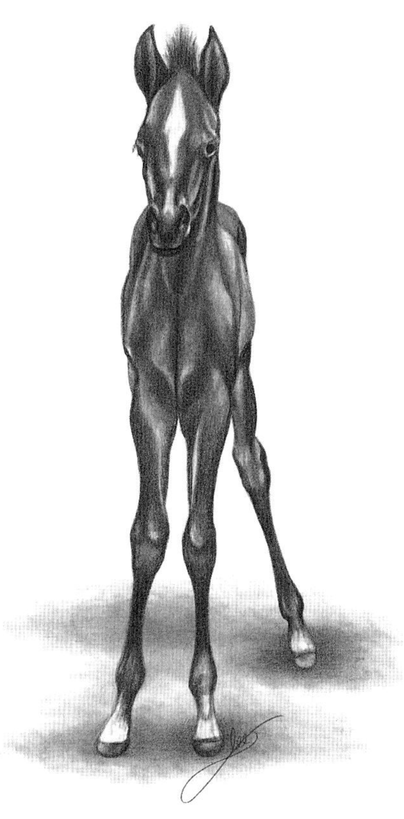

This shows the wobbly lankiness of a very young colt. To keep their balance, they must spread their legs apart. This view is a good example of foreshortening.

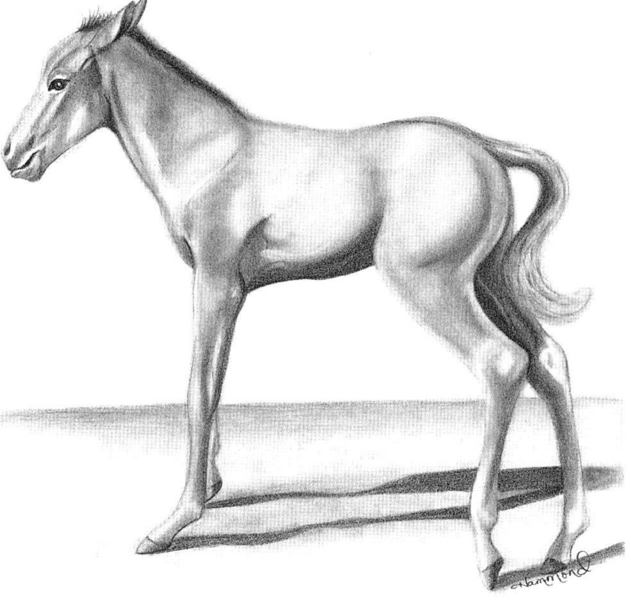

This youngster is more developed, looking more like an adult. Look for the five elements of shading on the roundness of its body.

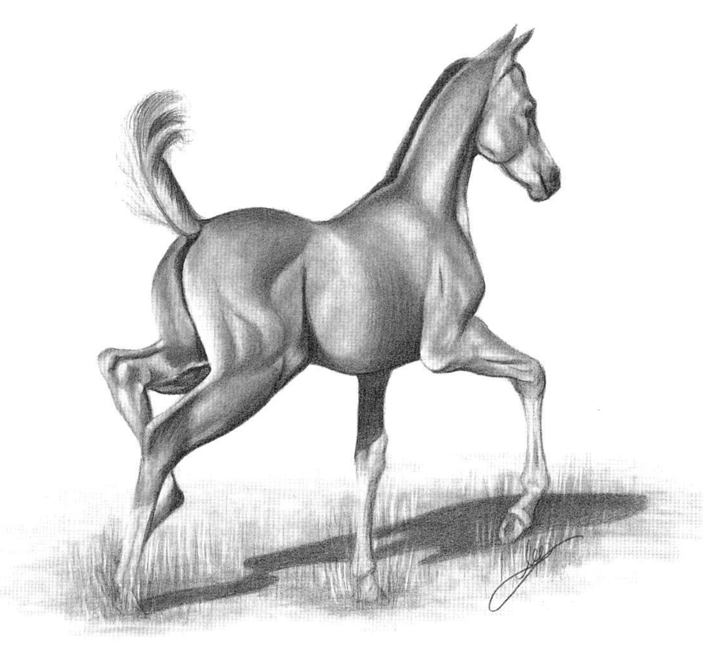

This frisky pose was enhanced by the shadow underneath. It gives the drawing a greater sense of motion.

Chapter Thirteen

Colors and Markings

As with many other animal species, horses come in many colors and variations. Their markings can range from tiny spots to huge areas of color. They can be light or dark, or a speckled combination of both. This chapter will give you some practice and understanding of how to capture that look in your drawings.

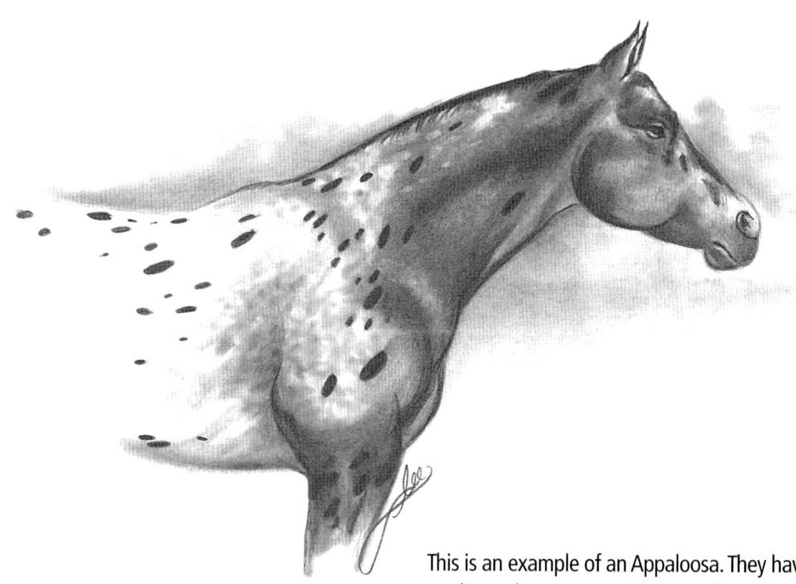

This is an example of an Appaloosa. They have markings that are a combination of mottled areas, solid colors and spots. They are most recognized for being darker in the front than the back, and having spots on their rumps. To draw a horse like this, I create the shape and contour areas first, like the face and shading of the neck. Then, I create the mottled appearance using a dirty tortillion and a circular stroke. This keeps it looking subtle. For the final detail, I draw in all of the dark spots.

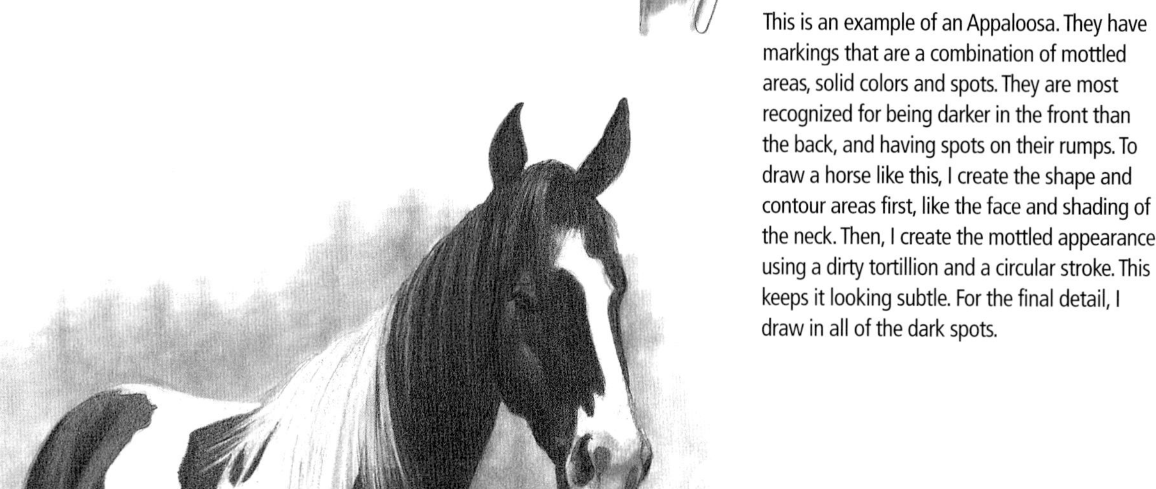

This beautiful horse is a good example of a "Paint." The markings are extreme in their contrasts, making it look like they were painted on. Even the mane is two-toned. When drawing a horse like this, it is harder to make the contours of the body show up in the dark areas. It is necessary to lift some highlights, to keep those areas from appearing flat.

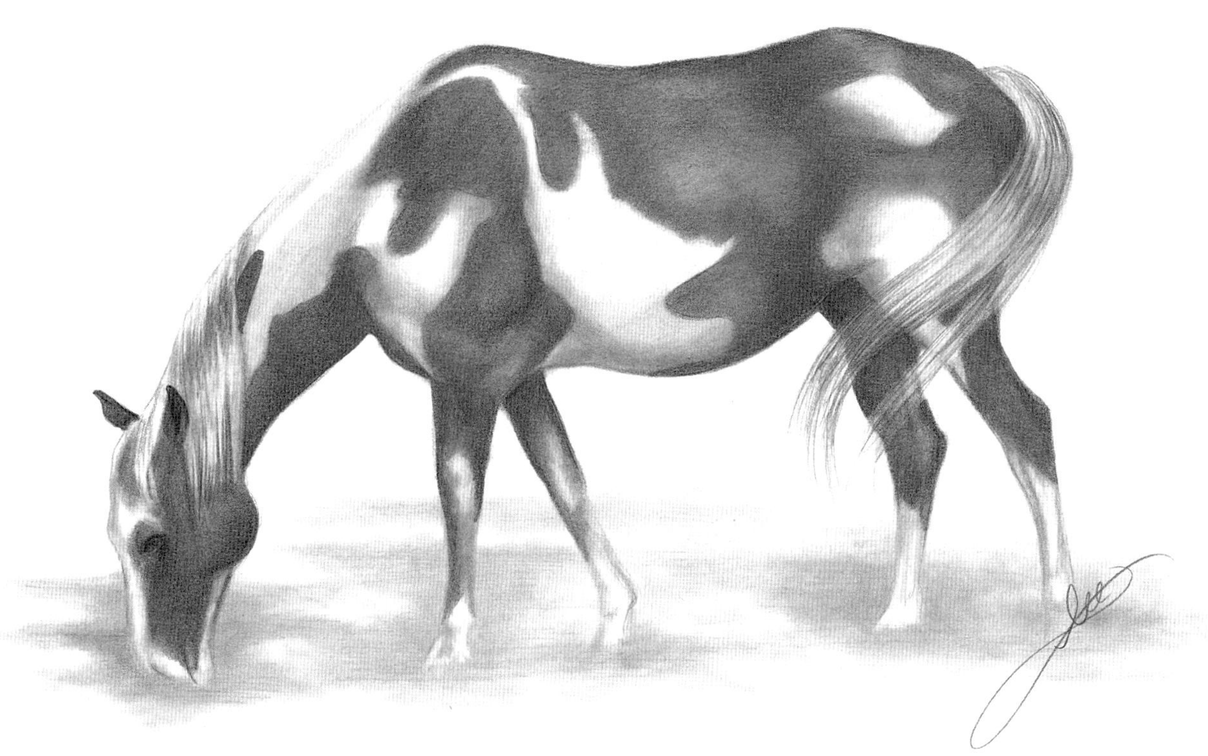

This horse is another example of a Paint. The colors and shapes of its marking make this a beautiful horse. A horse's markings are unique to each horse and will differ with each individual. Look in books and magazines where you will find a wide range of colorations and markings from which to practice.

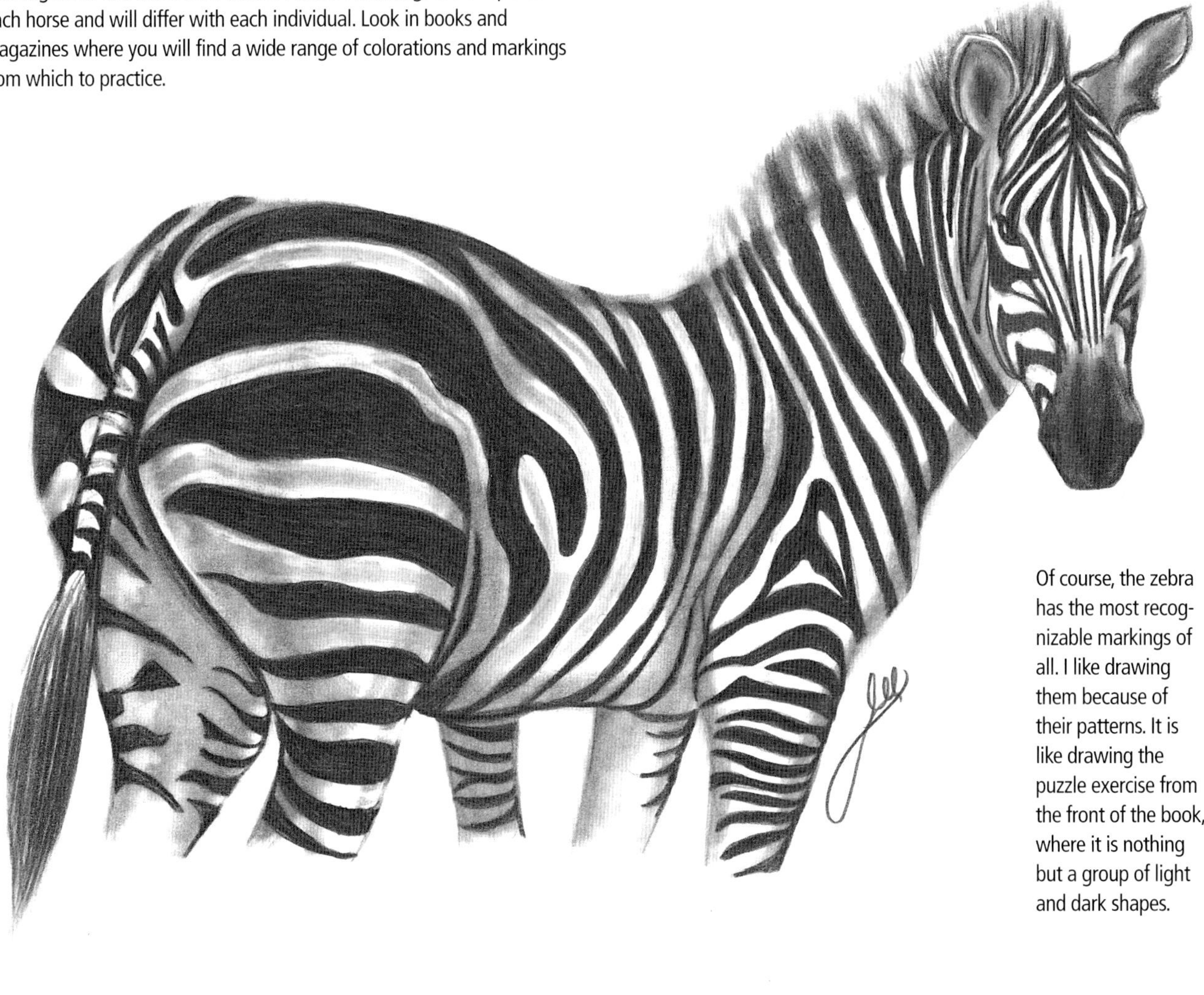

Of course, the zebra has the most recognizable markings of all. I like drawing them because of their patterns. It is like drawing the puzzle exercise from the front of the book, where it is nothing but a group of light and dark shapes.

Chapter Fourteen

Drawing the Horse in Motion

Until now, we have been drawing horses in fairly relaxed positions and circumstances. Now let's study the horse in motion, and see how the principles apply.

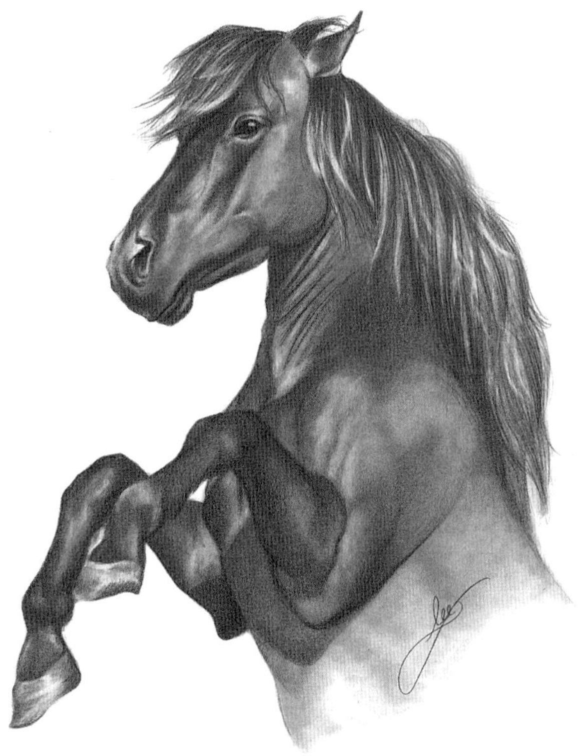

This is good example of a rearing horse. It was a good study for practicing drawing the legs and mane. This drawing was also the one I used to create the unicorn and Pegasus. Compare the three, and you will see how different each one looks.

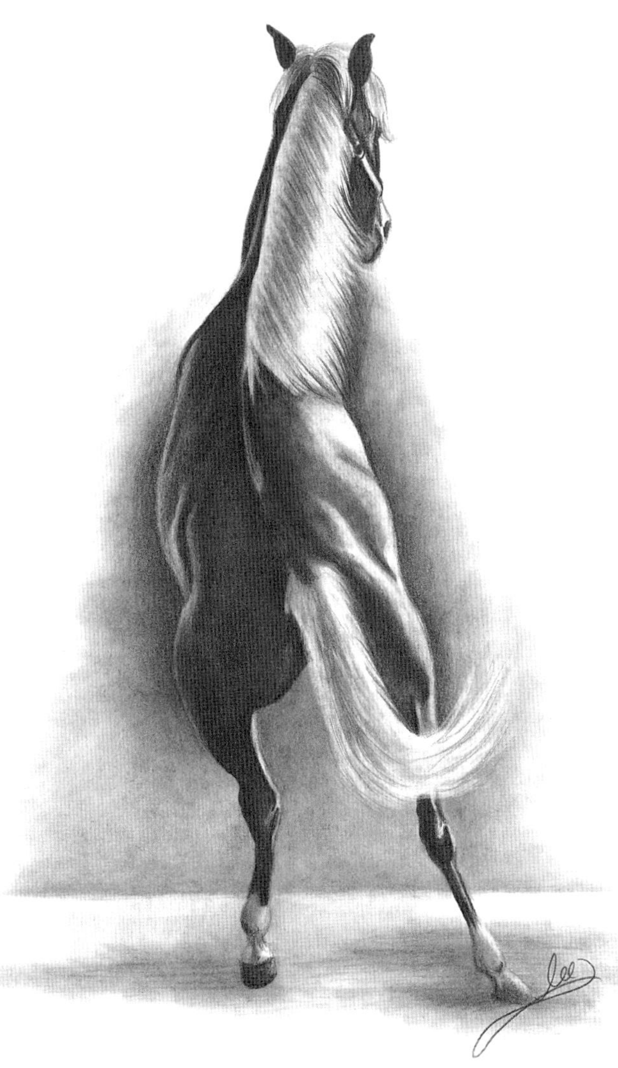

This pose is a good example of what a horse looks like in motion. The rearing horse is illuminated by backlighting, causing the light edges along its sides. You can also see the light reflecting down the sides of the legs. To enhance this, I placed the dark background around the horse for contrast. There is also contrast between the dark body and the light mane and tail. Look for the bands of light, which create the curvature of the hair. I used quick pencil strokes to replicate the look of hair.

Look at the tilt of the body. Can you see how it leans to the left? The bend of the legs shows that this horse is springing forward. The shadow underneath gives solidity to the drawing, giving the horse a foundation to stand on. You can almost feel the movement of this horse by looking at this drawing.

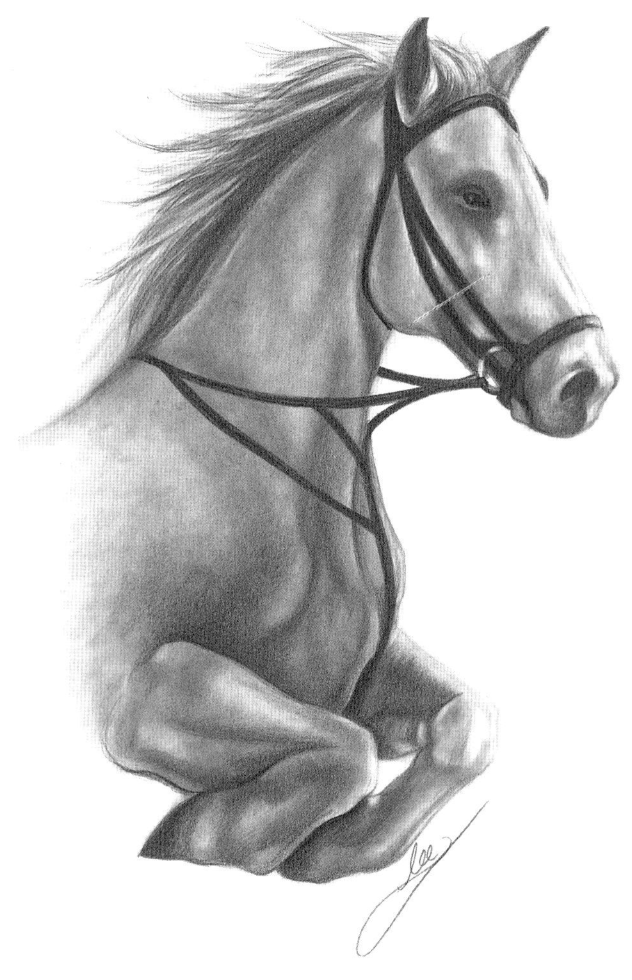

This is a similar pose to the one of the rearing horse on the previous page. But look at the differences in the pose of the legs. The legs being curled in like this means the horse is jumping, not rearing up. The bridle and reins tell us that it has a rider as well. The mane flowing back gives this drawing a real feeling of motion. This pose could easily be used as a model for a merry-go-round or a horsy swing.

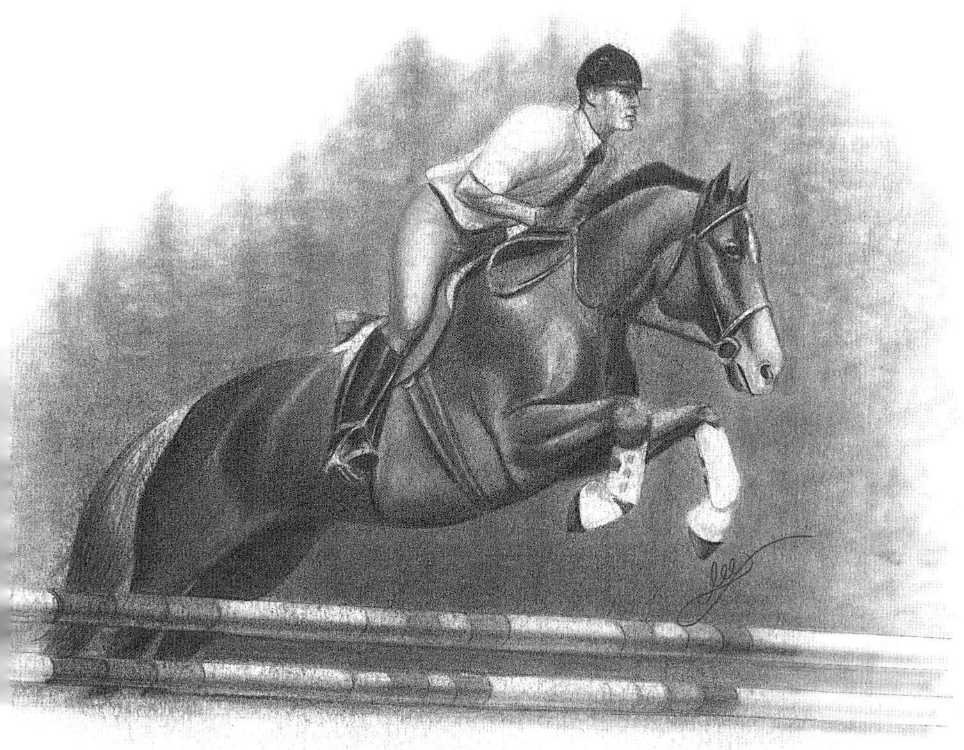

This is what the jumping horse would look like in its entirety. The outstretched hind legs further enhance the feeling of movement. Look at how the rider is leaning forward, mimicking the angle of the horse. You can almost feel the jump yourself. This is what a good illustration should do. Once again, I have used the dark background as a tool for making the light areas stand out. Because of this, the rider's shirt has a definite light source.

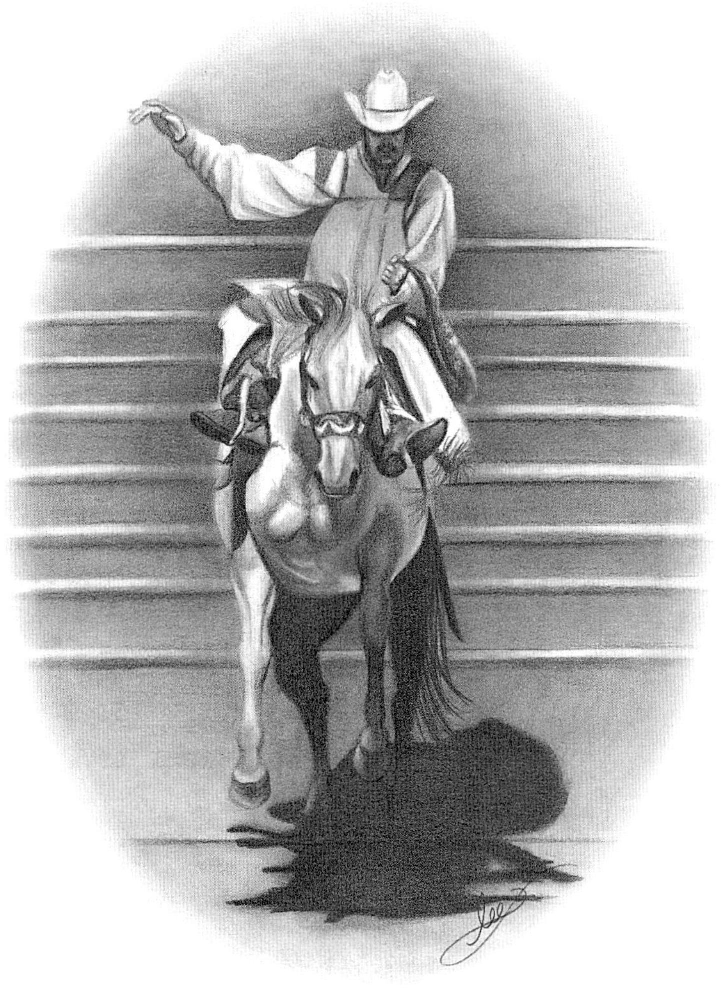

This rodeo scene shows the horse bursting forth, ready for action! The extreme lighting situation of this pose gives it a lot of appeal. Look at how the bright light areas contrast against the dark, creating patterns. The hind legs of the horse are so dark you see no details. They look like silhouettes. To draw this, I looked at those areas by squinting my eyes, and reducing them to just inanimate shapes. It made it much easier to draw.

To finish the drawing and further the visual impact, I drew in the fence rails. This helped set the scene of the rodeo. The horizontal positioning of the rails contrasts with the vertical movement of the horse, leading your eye to the horse and rider. I blended the background into an oval for a more interesting composition.

Photo reference used provided by Cyndi West.

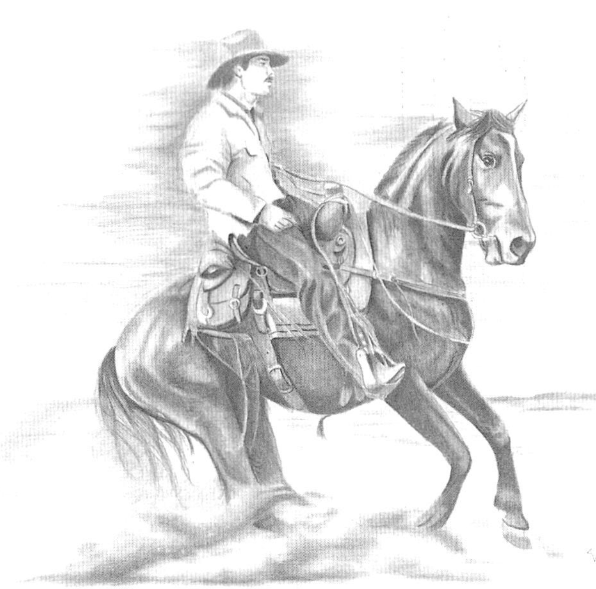

Look at how my student used the streaked background to aid in the illusion of movement here. The straight, inward tilt of the legs shows that the horse is skidding to a stop, and kicking up dust as it does.

Drawing by Cyndi West.

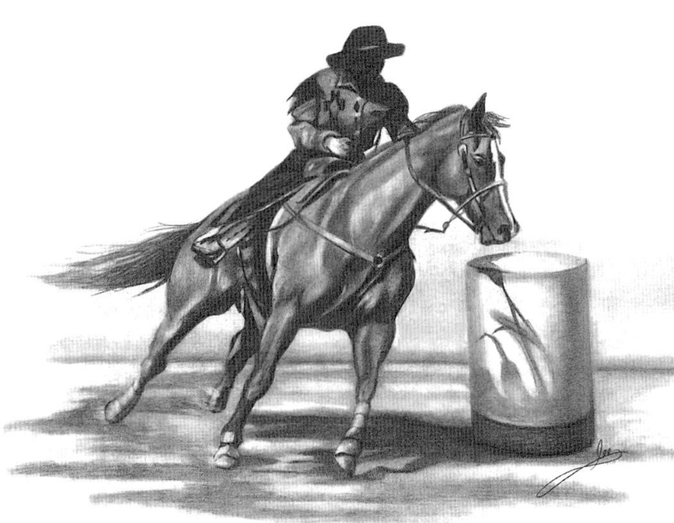

This horse is also kicking up dust as it makes the turn around the barrel. The extreme tilt of the horse, and the shadow coming out from it, makes this drawing appear full of action.

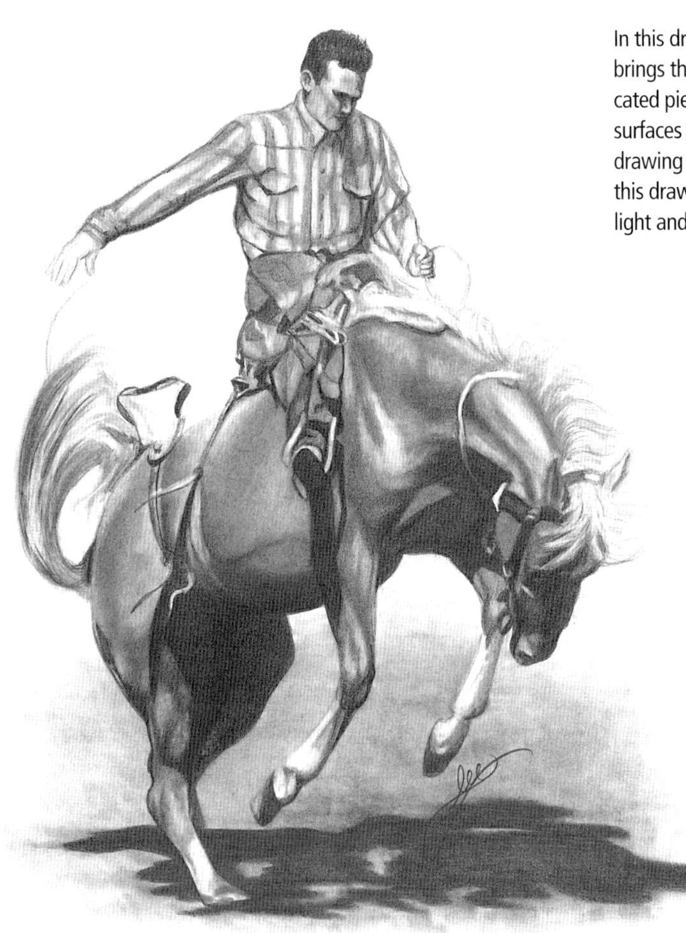

In this drawing, notice how the shadow below brings the drawing to life. This was a complicated piece, involving a lot of overlapping surfaces and intense lighting. For practice drawing extreme contrasts, place a graph over this drawing, and look at it just as patterns of light and dark.

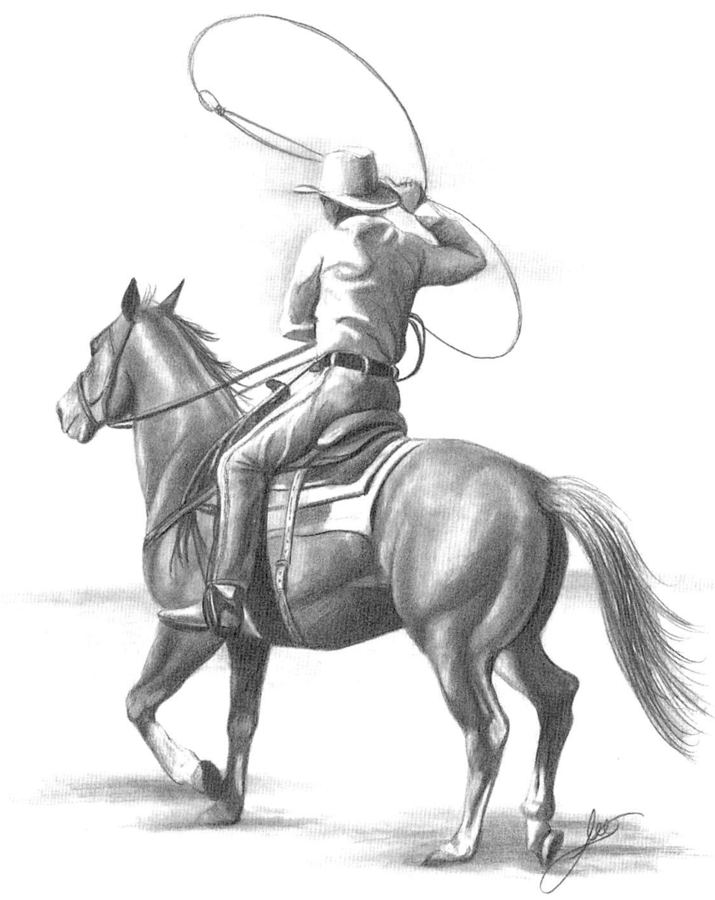

This drawing has a lot of direct sunlight illuminating the subjects. I like the patterns created on the shirt and pants of the rider. The action of the horse here is much less extreme than the bronco rider, making you look more at the movement of the rider's arm and rope.

CONCLUSION

As I drew the pictures for this book and typed the words of the manuscript, I was flooded with childhood memories of growing up in Lincoln, Nebraska. In my first book, *Lifelike Portraits from Photographs*, I included this drawing, and I'd like to show it again.

My love of horses is due to the fun times I had at Bob DeVoogd's horse stable. I spent countless hours there, up to the time I was an adult. To this day, I can still feel the sunshine, smell the hay and hear the sound of Bob's voice.

The most valuable thing you can gain from art is the enjoyment of doing it. It doesn't matter if your art hangs in galleries, or wins competitions, if the process makes you unhappy. I hope you find the same joy in it as I do. I've drawn every day for almost forty years, and I never tire of it!

Practice is truly the key to any success, so draw every day. Research pictures and references to practice from, and take your own photographs whenever possible. To draw well, you must "know" your subject, and be able to really "see" and study the shapes.

From the bottom of my heart, I wish you tremendous success!!

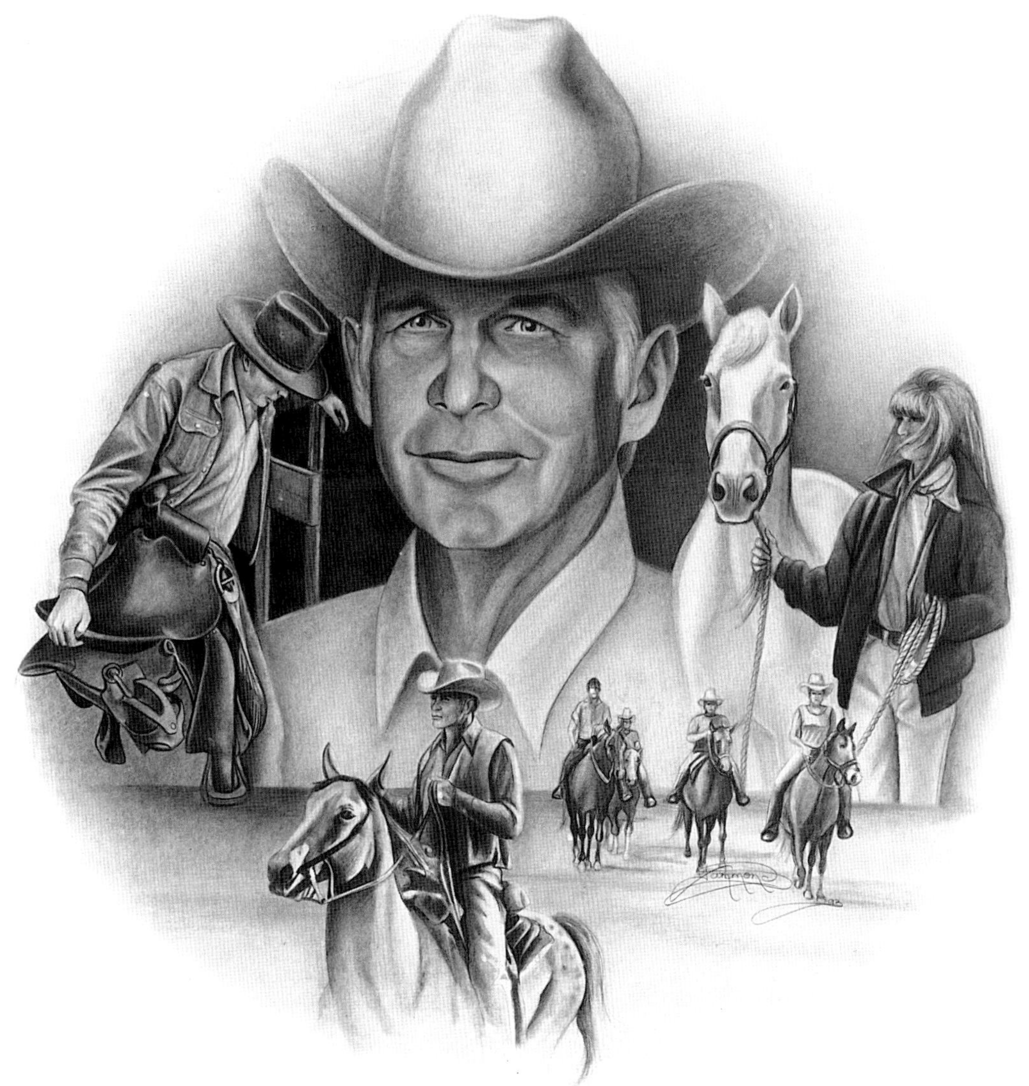

In memory of Bob DeVoogd and the Flying D Stables, Lincoln, Nebraska.

Good Luck!

The End!

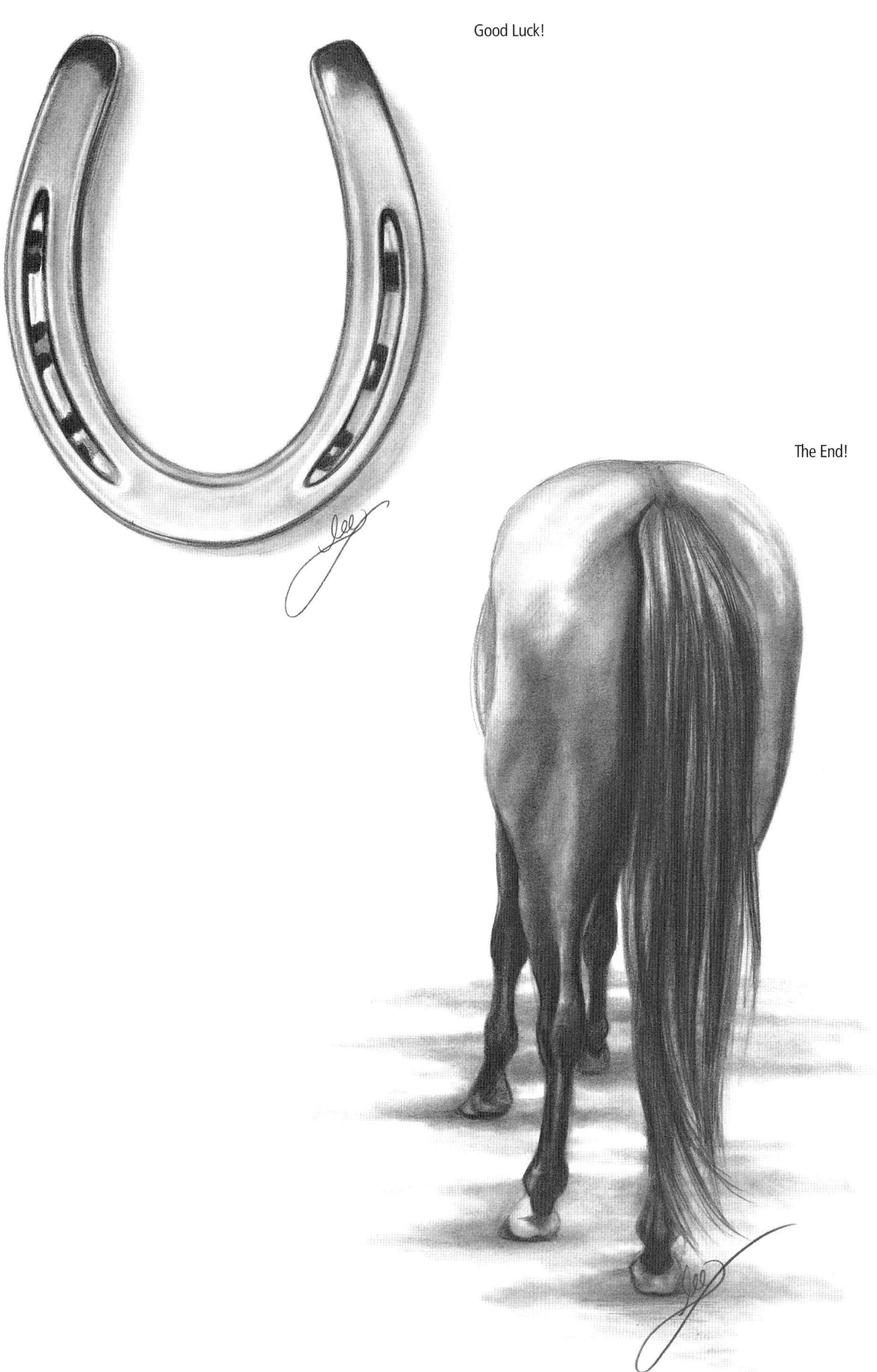

INDEX